HISTORY AND ENGLISH IN THE PRIMARY SCHOOL

Exploiting the links

Edited by Pat Hoodless

London and New York

First published 1998
by Routledge
11 New Fetter Lane, London EC4P 4EE

Simultaneously published in the USA and Canada
by Routledge
29 West 35th Street, New York, NY 10001

Typeset in Garamond by Keystroke, Jacaranda Lodge, Wolverhampton
Printed and bound in Great Britain by TJ International Ltd, Padstow, Cornwall

British Library Cataloguing in Publication Data
A catalogue record for this book is available from the British Library

Library of Congress Cataloging in Publication Data
History and English in the primary school : exploiting the links /
[edited by] Pat Hoodless
p.   cm.
Includes bibliographical references and index.
1. History—Study and teaching (Elementary)—Great Britain.
2. English language—Study and teaching (Elementary)—Great Britain.
3. Language arts (Elementary)—Great Britain. 4. Curriculum
planning—Great Britain. I. Hoodless, Pat, 1947– .
LB1582.G7H57   1998
372.89'044—dc21   98–23386
CIP

ISBN 0–415–16703–5

CONTENTS

CONTENTS

LIST OF FIGURES

LIST OF TABLES

NOTES ON CONTRIBUTORS

Janice Adams is currently Key Stage 1 co-ordinator at Didsbury Road Primary School, Stockport. She has taught in nurseries and schools in Manchester, Salford, Sheffield and The Netherlands and has also worked for six years as a lecturer in early years education at Didsbury School of Education, Manchester. She has an MA in education from the Open University.

Gill Bicknell has worked as a nursery nurse for ten years. She has recently completed a BA course in primary education and a primary Post-Graduate Certification in Education (PGCE) course at the Manchester Metropolitan University. She is currently teaching reception children at the Church of England School of the Resurrection, Manchester.

Joan Blyth trained primary teachers for many years and during the past decade has organised in-service courses for teachers on historical topics. She has written several books for teachers on primary history, including *History in Primary Schools*, *History 5 to 11* and (with Pat Hughes) *Using Written Sources in Primary History*.

Christine Cooper is a Senior Lecturer in history at the University College of St Martin, Lancaster. She has over twenty years' teaching experience and has taught the whole primary age range. Currently she is working with trainee teachers and is particularly interested in the links that can be established between history and English.

Hilary Cooper is currently head of the research programme in the Education Department at the University College of St Martin, Lancaster. She has spent many years as a class teacher in primary schools; her doctoral research, undertaken as a class teacher, investigated young children's thinking in history. She has published widely in this field, including the books *Teaching History* and *History in the Early Years*.

Kath Cox is a former primary school teacher who is now Senior Lecturer and co-ordinator of history curriculum courses at Liverpool Hope University

College. She is co-ordinator of the Hope Early Years Forum, a primary OFSTED inspector and a registered nursery inspector. She is co-author of teaching materials for children and teachers, including *Early Years History: An Approach Through Story*, *Starting History* and *History Through Photographs*.

Julie Davies was a primary teacher and head teacher for thirteen years, after graduating in history from Cardiff University. She presently teaches at Manchester Victoria University and is responsible for teaching primary history as well as English to pre-service students. She is the author of several papers on children's reading, attitudes to school and their self-esteem. She has a particular interest in the teaching of reading.

Amanda Donoghue is a newly qualified teacher, working in a Key Stage 2 class. She recently qualified as a primary teacher on the Primary Postgraduate Course at Manchester Victoria University, where she was an outstanding student and winner of the Charles Withers Memorial Prize.

Alan Farmer is head of history at the University College of St Martin, Lancaster. He has taught in a variety of primary and secondary schools, has done considerable INSET work in Lancashire, Cumbria and the Isle of Man and is presently a member of the Primary History National Committee. His research interests are in American history and the teaching of history, and he has published numerous books and articles.

Liz Grugeon is Senior Lecturer in English in primary education at De Montfort University, Bedford. She leads the research team 'Children learning through language', which is studying the extent to which children learn to use the specialist discourse of subject disciplines.

Penelope Harnett taught in infant, junior and middle schools before her appointment at the University of the West of England, Bristol, where she is Senior Lecturer in Primary Education and Research Fellow. She is a member of the editorial team for Ginn Primary History and has developed history resources for teachers, including *Curriculum Bank History*. Her research has investigated children's understanding in history, with a particular focus on the interpretation of visual sources. She is currently researching the development of the history curriculum in primary schools and teachers' views on history. She is Editor of *Primary History*.

Pat Hoodless is a former primary school teacher and has worked in several different local education authorities after graduating in history from London University. She has a master's degree in education from Liverpool University and is now Senior Lecturer in history and education at Didsbury School of Education, the Manchester Metropolitan University, with responsibility for courses in history and primary history teaching.

She has written articles and papers on children's learning in history and is the author of *Time and Timelines in the Primary School*.

Pat Hughes is a former primary school teacher and is now Senior Lecturer in Education at Liverpool Hope University and an OFSTED inspector. She is the author of education books on history and English: *Reading Skills at Key Stage 1 and Key Stage 2*, *Primary History* and *Using Written Sources in Primary History*.

Pat Nulty graduated from the University of York with a degree in history and English literature and has taught throughout the primary age range. Previously history co-ordinator in a large Cheshire primary school, she is currently teaching a Key Stage 1 class and is curriculum co-ordinator for arts. She was recently awarded a master's degree in education from University College Chester for studies related to primary school English and history.

Allan Redfern is a committee member of the Oral History Society and has been involved in oral history based research since the 1970s. Since 1985 he has been actively involved in a range of primary school oral history projects with pupils between five and eleven. He has made numerous contributions on the subject of oral history in schools through articles and conference papers. He is the author of *Talking in Class: Oral History and the National Curriculum*.

John Sampson is Principal Lecturer in primary education at De Montfort University, Bedford, where he has responsibility for primary initial teacher education. He has a special interest in primary history and has written a number of history books for children and teachers. Prior to this he taught for sixteen years in primary schools in Inner London.

Eleni Yiannaki has been a research student for the project 'Children learning through language' while studying for her PhD degree. She has been responsible for the collection and analysis of classroom data. She is now teaching in a primary school in Surrey.

FOREWORD

History is pre-eminently a literary subject. The study of the past requires and fosters an extended vocabulary; the development of listening, speaking and reading skills; the ability to write carefully, coherently and, at least occasionally, at some length. High standards in history and high standards in literacy are necessarily intertwined. In the best primary school practice teachers have always recognised this – and have planned and taught accordingly.

This is not simply an acknowledgement that history provides a suitable practice ground. Literacy demands more than the mastery of a set of language skills. It requires knowledge, access to those frames of reference which enable communication between author and reader, speaker and listener. Grasping the point, seeing the implication, recognising the allusion, following the argument – all depend crucially upon being able to give meaning to what is read or heard. Mere recognition of the words does not constitute under-standing. In teaching, therefore, our aim must be to establish both the necessary skills and the necessary network of information, to develop what has sometimes been identified as 'cultural literacy'.

History has an essential, not a subordinate, role to play here. So much of any language, the concepts it embodies, the modes of expression it employs, draws upon a shared cultural inheritance.

Given the current uncertainties which hover over the primary school curriculum, this book is a timely and important contribution to exploring the links there must be between history and English if we are to enable children to become genuinely literate. We will be selling them short if what we offer as literacy is too narrowly conceived.

JOHN HAMER, former HMI and specialist
adviser for history to OFSTED

PREFACE

It has been a long-standing concern shared by many professionals in education that the teaching of history and English should be related in the school curriculum. History is above all others a literary, language-based subject and should be treated as such. It provides an ideal context in which the learning and reinforcement of language skills may take place, since the skills involved in learning history are inextricably linked with language use. No greater opportunity is provided for the use of the imagination than in the reading of historical sources and historical literature, and in the creative act of recreating the past in writing. The study of history, moreover, fosters critical awareness of what is heard and read and develops skill in raising questions about sources of information, essential in a modern, democratic society.

As we approach the year 2000, however, there is growing concern that there will be less time for history in the primary curriculum. The progress made over recent years in the extension and development of primary history may be lost in many schools now that the requirements of the National Curriculum have been waived in order to make more time available for the study of 'the basics'. Recent discussions with historians, teacher educators and classroom practitioners have confirmed the view that, in the near future at least, there is an even more pressing need for teachers to create opportunities for historical contexts and sources to be used in the teaching of English. The contributors to this book share the belief that such opportunities should be used to enhance the teaching of both subjects, providing a richness of experience along the road to literacy, without which our children's lives would be very dull indeed.

ACKNOWLEDGEMENTS

Cover illustration We would like to thank the British Library, London and the Bridgeman Art Library for permission to reproduce A scribe (probably Bede) writing, by Bede, Latin (Durham) Life and Miracles of St Cuthbert, (12th century).

Chapter 1 Gill Bicknell offers her thanks to the staff and pupils at both Peel Brow Grant Maintained Primary School and St Andrews Church of England Primary School in Bury, Greater Manchester.

Chapter 2 Pat Nulty would like to thank the parents, staff and children of Stockton Heath Primary School, Cheshire, for their support, and Jackie Smalley and Sue Flynn for their patience in deciphering her scrawl.

Chapter 3 Alan Farmer and Christine Cooper would like to thank Jonathan Cape for permission to reproduce the extract from *A History of the World in Ten and a Half Chapters* by Julian Barnes.

Chapter 5 Penelope Harnett thanks the St Albans Museum Service for permission to reproduce the picture of the interior of a Roman kitchen, and the National Portrait Gallery for permission to reproduce the portrait of Queen Elizabeth I.

Chapter 7 Pat Hoodless would like to offer thanks to BEd students at Didsbury School of Education for spending time talking to children about time, and to the staff and children of Stockton Heath County Primary School, Cheshire, and Didsbury Road Primary School, Stockport.

Chapter 8 Julie Davies and Amanda Donoghue would like to acknowledge permission from Domino Books (Wales) Ltd, Swansea, to reproduce the drawing of Queen Victoria's Coronation and the drawing of the one penny stamp from *Victorian Britain: a Master File, Key Stages 2 and 3*, general editors D.C. Perkins and E.J. Perkins, illustrations by Anthony James; also for extracts taken from page 42 of the same volume, 'A Victorian Success Story: The Great Exhibition, 1851', and adaptation of page 78, 'A Victorian Dictionary Quiz' (Not photocopiable). Also to Ginn and Co. for permission to reproduce the extract from *Mary Seacole* by Sylvia Collicott.

Chapter 9 Joan Blyth would like to thank Jean Matthews and the pupils and staff of St Hilda's Church of England Aided Primary School, Stretford, Greater Manchester, and the pupils and staff of Didsbury Road Primary School, Stockport, Manchester. Document 10 from *Poverty and Vagrancy in Tudor England*, by J.F. Pound, is reprinted by permission of Addison Wesley Longman Ltd.

Chapter 10 John Sampson, Elizabeth Grugeon and Eleni Yiannaki would like to thank class 5P, summer 1996, Goldington Middle School, Bedford, for their part in contributing to this chapter.

Chapter 11 Hilary Cooper would like to thank the five students who worked on this project during their vacation: Sarra Thorne, Laura Jones, Alex Fisher, Anne Brain and Alex Hayes; their class teacher, Pat Etches who was such a support and inspiration to them and her class at Syramongate School, Kendal, Cumbria.

Chapter 12 Janice Adams would like to offer grateful thanks to the children and staff of the British School in The Netherlands and of Didsbury Road Primary School, Stockport.

INTRODUCTION

Exploiting the links between history and English

Pat Hoodless

Children learn about the past in many ways, frequently from television, films or from family excursions. They also discuss past events during family conversations and in school. What characterises history for most of us, however, is the visual imagery that goes with the past. If asked to think about the Tudors, for instance, I expect many people would suddenly find appearing in their mind's eye a version of some portrait of Henry VIII or Elizabeth I. However, what provides meaning for all these random images and impressions is the thinking, talking, reading and writing which accompanies them. Without this vital input from language our impressions would remain random and probably quite meaningless.

Language is the symbolic medium through which we can communicate our understanding of abstractions, of which the past is a part. In modern western societies, history is largely retained, recorded and transmitted through the medium of language. Language and the use of English plays a major role in any kind of historical activity, from a pupil carrying out a history-based task in a primary school, to an academic or professional historian researching and writing about their subject. Not surprisingly, therefore, as many reflective practitioners know, the teaching and learning of history relies to a considerable extent upon the use of language and, in the UK, the simultaneous teaching of English.

Different models of history teaching all rely heavily on language use, both by teacher and pupils (Husbands 1996). Essential skills in history often depend directly upon skill in the use of language, increasingly so as the learner moves on through the education system. At any level, speaking, listening, reading, reference skills and writing frequently all play a part in the process of historical enquiry, the use of sources, historical thought and understanding and in the communication of historical findings. Indeed, it would be difficult to develop in children the process skills of history

1

without the extensive use of this entire range of language skills. Historical content similarly requires specialist language knowledge and skill in manipulating and communicating factual information. Whatever style of teaching or learning in history is adopted, whether process or content focused, the links between history and English are inevitable, natural and inseparable.

The value of history in the teaching of English is that it provides a meaningful context within which the child may work with interest and understanding. History lessons and historical activities can promote enthusiasm, curiosity and a natural desire to investigate, encouraging the child to read for enjoyment and information. History also has the potential to stimulate writing, since it provides colourful material for the child to use to develop imagination, investigative strategies and a wide variety of styles of writing. History also provides an endless number of models on which written work may be based. This belief is grounded in the language variation theory of Halliday (1975), Britton (1970) and Carter (1990), who argue that language is embedded in culture and is created for specific purposes and audiences. History is particularly well placed to provide a full range of contexts for different language functions and it also has the potential to develop both precision and creativity in the child's work. In saying this, I do not suggest that history should be viewed primarily as a tool to support literacy. My argument is that, since history cannot be practised without considerable use of English, then we need to acknowledge this fact by stating precisely our intentions in the concurrent teaching of both subjects, each of which serves to enhance the development of the other. Oral history and speaking and listening are inextricably linked and depend entirely upon each other. The use of written historical sources depends in varying degrees upon thought, discussion and reading. Similarly, the communication of historical findings and interpretations relies upon either speaking or writing or both. If progression in learning is planned for both language and history, then the scarce time available in the primary curriculum can be very profitably used.

A broadly based rationale has supported this view over a number of years, first through a clear line of development in both academic and professional writing. Early literature on research into language and thought (Vygotsky 1962) demonstrated the essential role played by language as 'mediator' in the thinking process. It enables reflection to occur between actions, and consequently has considerable relevance to learning in history. These findings have been explicitly applied by Bruner (1960) to work in the humanities. His interest in 'how incoming signals are sorted out and organised' led him to intensive study of inferential thinking, a key part of the process of historical enquiry. Bruner's three forms of representation, the iconic, enactive and symbolic, as Nichol (1997) has expertly shown, all occur in historical enquiry, but the most extensively used is the 'symbolic', or linguistic, form.

There is now a general consensus that language is a key element in the learning of history, for instance, Cooper's (1995) discussion of the social dimension in language acquisition. She argues that discussion and group interaction contribute both to linguistic capability and historical expertise. Her recent classroom research has highlighted history as the provider of an excellent context in which to develop skills in discussion.

Official documentation has repeatedly emphasised the significance of the links between English and other curricular areas. As far back as 1921 the Newbolt Report discussed the question of 'the relation of English to other studies' (Board of Education 1921: 1). Since then there have been numerous official documents voicing a similar concern. The Bullock Report (DES 1975), NCC (DfE 1995), SCAA (1997b), the National Literacy Strategy (DfEE 1998), and the Nuffield History Project (Fines and Nichol 1997) have all in differing degrees returned to this issue. SCAA, in its recent publications *History and the Use of Language* (1997a) and *English and the Use of Language Requirement in Other Subjects* (1997b), gives examples of the links which teachers should be using. It states:

> history provides the stimulus of studying people and events in the past on local, national and global scales, as the context for language work. The development of children's historical knowledge, understanding and skills is closely linked to their ability to use language.
>
> (SCAA 1997b: 1)

The National Literacy Strategy includes the following in its definition of literate primary children. They should:

- know, understand and be able to write in a range of genres in fiction and poetry, and *understand and be familiar with some of the ways in which narratives are structured . . .* ;
- *understand, use and be able to write a range of non-fiction text*s;
- be interested in books, read with enjoyment and evaluate and justify preferences.

> (DfEE 1998: 3; italics added)

I would argue that all of these points apply equally to the study of history, while those in italics correspond to skills fundamental in historical study. There is occasionally specific reference to links with history, 'historical stories and short novels (ibid.: 67) and numerous literacy skills are identified in 'The Termly Objectives' (ibid.: section 2) as having a direct link with those used in historical study, such as :

> Pupils should be taught:
> - to understand and use the terms *fact* and *opinion*; and to begin to

distinguish the two in reading and other media (p. 39) [text level work];

- to use reading to investigate conditionals, e.g. using *if . . . then, might, could, would,* and their uses, e.g. in deduction, speculation, supposition (p. 53) [sentence level work];
- to understand that the meanings of words have changed over time (p. 53) [word level work].

Recent circulars to teacher training institutions have highlighted the need for newly qualified teachers to focus on developing literacy wherever possible (DfEE 1998). Clearly there is the opportunity to involve language-based subjects such as history to a considerable extent in doing this as is acknowledged in *Maintaining breadth and balance at Key States 1 and 2* (QCA 1998). Conversely, there is a clear need for the development of understanding specialist vocabulary and different kinds of texts in history. Chris Burns (1997), for example, writing in a recent edition of *Language and Literacy News*, provides a detailed example of work at text, sentence and word level on extending children's understanding of the use of non-fiction books by creating a catalogue to be used for work in history.

However, the most important justification for exploiting the natural, inseparable links between history and English is the fact that many classroom teachers find these very evident and also very useful as mutually supportive elements within their teaching programmes. This book, therefore, aims to clarify ways in which the two subjects are mutually supportive and to suggest strategies and techniques for teaching both subjects concurrently.

It includes recent work by classroom teachers and small-scale research into the links between English and history. Each chapter considers how the subjects are mutually supportive within a particular aspect of the primary history curriculum. It is argued throughout the book that teaching/learning objectives need to be set for both subject areas, in the acknowledgement that both will be addressed within particular activities. There is a need to recognise the value of teaching strategies which ensure progression in both history and English. Planning, organisational and assessment strategies at classroom level all need to allow for the application and development of skills in both history and English. Each chapter, in its own way, offers guidance and ideas for implementing such aims. While no chapters refer specifically to issues such as planning for children with Special Educational Needs or the incorporation of the use of information and communications technology, these are referred to where they occur naturally throughout the book.

Contributors give accounts of classroom activities and suggest sources and ideas which might be used in work on history, providing illustrations and examples across the history curriculum. They consider both the value of certain activities as well as the problems involved in carrying them out. Some include examples and analysis of children's talk or writing and consider the implications of their findings for teaching and learning.

Speaking and listening

The spoken word, both heard and uttered, is the foundation upon which other literacy skills are built: 'Young children absorb many aspects of the "rules" of their mother tongue even as they learn to talk' (Carter 1990: 46). Consequently, much of children's progress in writing is based upon knowledge about language learned first through the spoken word. Children assimilate and adapt to new knowledge and schemas first through this symbolic medium, hence the crucial significance of discussion in the learning of new historical content and ideas. Opportunities for speaking and listening are broad and varied in history and have been discussed by many, including Allan Redfern, John Fines, Alan Farmer and Hilary Cooper. These opportunities include, among many others: oral history; listening to stories being read or told; listening to broadcasts, tapes or computer programs; group and class discussions about artefacts and pictures; visits to historic sites or museums; listening to visiting speakers; drama, simulation and role play; or presenting work in class or in assembly. In a world dominated by the visual image, however, speaking and listening skills are not always easy to develop in young children. The first five chapters propose a variety of approaches to this task, some well tried and others fairly innovative.

Reading

As in the study of English, the use of books, documents and other source materials written in a variety of genres is fundamental to historical enquiry. However, the conceptual demands upon the reader of historical writing are frequently very great, requiring an understanding of a bygone age in which different values and assumptions underlay interactions and events. The demands upon the child's understanding are also considerable in areas such as awareness of time and the manipulation of time in literature. This is particularly true when using primary source materials which were written for an adult audience. Similarly, the technical demands made upon the primary school child's reading ability in documents and non-fiction history books are often considerable. There is, indeed, a high degree of mismatch beween children's general reading levels and the readability levels in much historical text and school non-fiction books. This is an increasingly difficult problem, exacerbated by the decreasing standards in literacy which appears to have occurred in primary schools in recent years.

Much recent research has advocated the use of literature in teaching history. Advocates of this as an approach include Kath Cox, Pat Hughes, Joan Blyth and Alan Farmer, among many others. Key areas, such as continuity and change, interpretation and time, can be addressed in the primary school, using literary sources. Time concepts can be explored and developed through the use of story and literature. Fiction and poetry provide valuable contextual backgrounds for on-going work in history topics or themes. Literature can also support and illustrate key concepts in history, such as continuity and change, chronology or causation.

Non-fiction texts, such as primary written sources, can be used very successfully to extend children's literacy skills and to challenge the very able children in the junior school. There is a very broad range of source material, from posters, which use only a limited amount of text, to documents of great complexity. Careful selection and sequencing of such documents can provide an increasingly challenging set of learning objectives, both for history and for reading. Chapters 6–9 look at some of these approaches to the teaching and use of reading in history.

Writing

Recent work by Husbands (1996) and Counsell (1997) has highlighted the exceptional potential of history to provide a variety of different genres in which children may write and audiences for whom they may write. Using sources from history as stimulus material, children can produce inventories, reports, narrative accounts, letters, newspaper pages, questionnaires, books, stories, interviews and descriptions. They can be guided and their efforts scaffolded in a number of ways, such as the 'writing frames', of which some excellent examples appear in both Counsell (1997) and Nichol (1997). Lomas (1990) points out the important links between English and history in terms of creativity. Although the use of imagination and creativity are essential elements in historical reconstruction they do not appear in the National Curriculum for history. Language permits the use of the imagination, enabling the child to engage in creative writing set within an historical framework. Chapters 10–12 consider teacher input and different historical stimuli as motivators, forms of scaffolding and models for children's own writing.

References

Blyth, J. and Hughes, P. (1997) *Using Written Sources in Primary History*, London: Hodder and Stoughton.
Board of Education (1921) *The Teaching of English in England*, London: HMSO.
Britton, J. (1970) *Language and Learning*, Harmondsworth: Penguin.
Bruner, J.S. (1960) *The Process of Education*, New York: Vintage.
Burns, C. (1997) 'Working Towards a Literacy Hour Framework (KS2)', *Language and Literacy News*, Autumn.
Carter, R. (ed.) (1990) *Knowledge about Language and the Curriculum*, London: Hodder and Stoughton.

Cooper, H. (1995) *The Teaching of History in Primary Schools: Implementing the Revised National Curriculum*, 2nd edn, London: David Fulton.

Counsell, C. (1997) *Analytical and Discursive Writing at KS3*, London: Historical Association.

Department for Education (DfE) (1995) *History in the National Curriculum*, London: HMSO.

Department for Education and Employment (DfEE) (1998) *Teaching: High Status, High Standards*, Circular 4/98, London: DfEE.

—— (1998) *The National Literacy Strategy Framework for Teaching*, London: DfEE.

Department of Education and Science (DES) (1975) *A Language for Life*, London: HMSO.

Fines, J. and Nichol, J. (1997) *The Nuffield History Project: Teaching Primary History*, London: Heinemann.

Halliday, M.A.K. (1975) *Learning How to Mean: Explorations in the Development of Language*, London: Arnold.

Husbands, C. (1996) *What is History Teaching? Language, Ideas and Meaning in Learning about the Past*, Buckingham: Open University Press.

Lomas, T. (1990) *Teaching and Assessing Historical Understanding*, London: Historical Association.

Nichol, J. with Dean, L. (1997) *History 7–11: Developing Primary Teaching Skills*, London: Routledge.

Qualifications and Curriculum Authority (QCA) (1998) *Maintaining breadth and balance at Key Stage 1 and 2*, Hayes, Middlesex: QCA Publications.

School Curriculum and Assessment Authority (1997a) *History and the Use of Language*, London: SCAA Publications.

—— (1997b) *English and the Use of Language Requirement in Other Subjects*, London: SCAA Publications.

Vygotsky, L.S. (1962) *Thought and Language*, New York: MIT Press.

Wray, D. and Medwell, J. (1991) *Literacy and Language in the Primary Years*, London: Routledge.

1

PEEL APPEAL

Talking about the locality with nursery and reception children

Gill Bicknell

Peel Tower is a dominant feature of the Ramsbottom landscape and for children who live in this area it never fails to bring a response. Ramsbottom is a small town of Victorian character situated in the Irwell Valley on the border of Bury in Greater Manchester. The tower was built approximately 150 years ago in memory of Sir Robert Peel, who was born in Bury and later became Prime Minister. He is remembered for repealing the corn laws and for forming the modern police force.

Local children talk readily about walking up Holcombe Hill to visit the monument, about the magnificent views from the top of the tower and about being able to see it from their houses. To young and old it is very impressive. It was with this ready-made historical attraction that I set about a project with nursery children and later, in more detail, with children in a reception class.

I was eager to develop children's oral language skills as history depends very heavily on the ability to provide accounts of the past and to describe them in detail. Children need sequencing skills to order past events, just as they need them when writing a story or instructions. In order to study history children need verbal reasoning skills to understand and explain how actions undertaken in the past can affect future events. Communication skills to clarify and express ideas are essential. Children need to be able to read about the past in a critical and meaningful way. It is difficult to separate the teaching of history and English and, as the National Curriculum recognises, the subjects overlap in many ways.

Researchers have already linked children's early language development to future success in reading and writing and see it as the root from which literacy grows. Frank Smith (1978) and Kenneth Goodman (1982) recognised that learning to talk and learning to read were achieved by children trying to make meaning from language. Wells (1986) recognised the link between language

8

experiences and children's emergent literacy skills. He found in his Bristol study that children who were read to from a young age did significantly better in their reading in later years. Halliday (1977) identifies seven different functions of language which he considers to have links with reading and writing. He claims that if children are familiar with these functions and use in oral language then they will have an advantage when using them in written language. They include:

- regulatory language – this controls the actions of others and enables the child to step out of play and become the narrator. In writing this function would be used to make appointments or to arrange meetings;
- interactional language – this allows children to 'get along' with other people and in writing would be used in letter writing;
- informative language – this communicates new information to other children and in writing would be employed in reports and newspaper articles;
- imaginative language – this allows children to participate in pretend play and forms the basis for future story or play writing;
- heuristic language – this is a questioning function of language which enables the child to seek information. It would form the basis of written enquiries;
- personal language – this allows children to make an opinion about issues and would be essential for diary or journal writing;
- instrumental language – this function satisfies a need and allows the child to request something. It would be necessary for writing orders or writing cheques.

In order to develop these functions I introduced activities with an historical focus which would facilitate their use.

Nursery children's talk

With children of pre-school age the interest in Peel Tower was exploited by arranging for the children to walk there for a summer picnic. They were told that this tower was built to remember a person called Peel who lived long ago and who was responsible for starting the first police force. This was particularly relevant to this group of children as the school and nearest main road were also named after Peel and in a way this information gave them a sense of identity with the area. They were told that Peel was born in Bury and spent his childhood in this area.

Upon reaching the tower, after a steep climb, children, adults and those who had visited the monument before were still surprised at the size. It is an impressive 128 feet high. They were asked questions to draw their attention to what it was made of and if the stones used looked like the stone used on their houses. They were able to observe the word 'Peel' which is engraved in the stone above the door to the tower. Unfortunately, our picnic was cut short by an unexpected downpour of rain and had to be finished off back at the nursery.

In the days that followed this trip the children drew pictures of the tower, made junk models of it and a collage of the tower and an old policeman.

During this time I was able to listen to their language and observe how this topic had enhanced their language development and at the same time encouraged an interest in the past. One child was heard to say:

I can't wait until my Mummy comes to tell her why it is called Peel Tower.

When she did arrive, he eagerly told her:

Mummy, that Peel Tower was called Peel Tower because a man started the police and that was his name.

A conversation between some children who were working on a collage of the tower was very revealing. They were talking about the shades of the sponge-printed collage pieces that were being used for the stones:

Child A: This tower is black. I think it is black.
Child B: Mine is black here and this one is nearly black.
Child A: I like this one black. It's been on the tower a long time and it's all dirty.
Child B: Black and dirty. My house isn't black and dirty is it?
Child A: No, your house wasn't built longest ago. My house wasn't built longest ago. I think this tower was.

Through listening to the children's talk, it was obvious that the project had certainly aroused an interest in the past and that the success of this was probably down to the fact that it was developed from a feature that was familiar to them.

The first child, who was eager to tell his mother about his recently acquired knowledge, was using very informative language which will be required in later years for reporting past incidents. He was able to construct a complex sentence with the use of the connective 'because'. This is an important part of language development as well as being a very desirable skill in history study as it is vital to conveying understanding in a subject.

Figure 1.1 A 'Peeler'

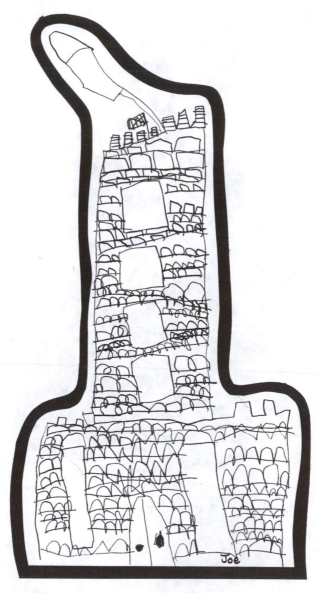

Figure 1.2 'Peel Tower': drawing by a nursery child

Clearly this child has begun to make causal links between events and has acquired the linguistic skill to express this understanding.

The children who were involved with the collage work were obviously influenced by the questions the adults had asked and through their talk had shown some sense of the past and some basic sense of chronology. They were fulfilling the National Curriculum requirements for Key Stage 1 where, in the Key Elements, children should learn to sequence events and begin to use phrases relating to the past. This, indeed, was the case when he used the term 'longest ago', although it was not grammatically correct. (See also Chapter 7, where similar findings occur, revealing that very young children know and use words to do with concepts such as time, but do not, at first, use them accurately.)

The talk of these nursery children corroborates the findings of Gordon Wells when he states:

> Language provides a means not only for acting in the world but also for reflecting on that action in an attempt to understand it. Initially, such reflection takes place through conversation – through dialogue with another more knowledgeable person. But gradually, if children have many positive experiences of this kind, they begin to be able to manage both roles for themselves. They come to be able to frame questions and interrogate their own experience in the search for an answer. In this way, language becomes a tool for thinking.
>
> (Wells 1986: 65)

I believe it was the stimulus of the visit directly linked to the follow-up activities that enabled the children to reflect on their experiences. Before and during the visit the concept of older, weathered stone had been initiated by adults who knew more about these facts. By reinforcing the concepts in the choice of collage materials it did indeed enable the children to discuss their experiences in search of meaning. This was done without any intervention from an adult. Wells's statement was very pertinent as these children had employed the use of talk for further understanding.

Reception children's talk

I felt this project with pre-school children had been successful in creating an interest in the past and I repeated the topic about the connections with Sir Robert Peel when working with a reception class in another Ramsbottom school. The school's long-term plans included a history/geography project on people who help us in the community. The school was also due to celebrate the 125th anniversary of its opening, so I thought this was an opportunity to look at the history of the police force and combine it with opportunities for language development. In order to address these combined objectives I decided to set up a role play area as a Victorian police station. I believe this type of structured play area is one of the best ways to develop children's language and historical awareness.

During role play, children are likely to use Halliday's language functions and in doing so will act out stories and situations. What better opportunity is there for practising those sequencing skills which were mentioned earlier, and to note the type of language use and functions of language promoted by such activities? Recent research has found that children's language in the role play area is more developed and more mature than in the normal classroom context. James Christie (1991: 33) refers to the work of Pellegrini when he states: 'The housekeeping areas have also been found to elicit the use of more imaginative and multifunctional language than other activity areas.' Role play encourages social interaction which is essential to language development, and the creation of an historical role play area helps to recreate an atmosphere of the past which is easy for the young child to absorb.

To set the scene, a police officer was invited into school to talk about his present-day work, uniform and equipment. When I later took in pictures of 'Charlies', 'Peelers' and later Victorian policemen, the children were very quick to spot similarities and differences. They listened to stories I created about the reasons for setting up a police force and this was enhanced by a 'Victorian' visitor who gave them a vivid account of pickpocketing. The children even had an opportunity to take part in this activity!

A 'Victorian police station' was therefore set up complete with top hats, truncheons, handcuffs and bars at the windows (Figures 1.3 and 1.4). The children were involved in the choice of equipment to be put in the police station and, after studying photographs of the Manchester Police Museum, agreed that there was no place in their role play area for a computer or a telephone! The children all wore Victorian costume on the actual anniversary, which helped to create an appropriate atmosphere. Once the excitement of having such an area had abated the children were observed in their play and the language was noted.

It soon became evident that some children were using this role play area to act out the story of *The Three Billy Goats Gruff*. Recent work in English had been to describe how the ugly troll looked and to use these descriptions to make 'wanted' posters. I suppose I should not have been too surprised because these children were exploring the familiar, and the ugly troll to them was a very real 'villain'. One conversation went as follows:

Child C: We must get this man. *(Pointing to a poster of a troll)*
Child D: Yes, let's see what he looks like.
Child C: We must get this bandit. He has red eyes, he has sharp claws, he has clothes that are broken. He has taken the gold. *(The children then proceed to walk around the room trying to find him)*

Figure 1.3 The Victorian police station role play area

The drama then developed when a third child volunteered to be the troll and was duly escorted to the police station where he was made to return the gold. The plot of the story was not terribly exciting, although I was interested in the descriptive language that was emerging, not only with these children but with other groups of children as well. The skill of gaining information from artefacts, pictures and photographs through the essential use of descriptive language involved both history and English.

From these observations I decided to introduce police record cards on which the children were encouraged to write descriptions of themselves and real and imaginary friends. This was highly successful, especially as there was a space on the cards for fingerprints! As the children's descriptive language was certainly developing, I thought it was an opportune time to introduce 'lost property' into the police station including a variety of Victorian and reproduction items. Amongst these items were old pennies, a flat iron, silver-framed photographs, a carpet beater, lace and a Victorian butter cooler.

I am aware that historical artefacts enable children to engage in first-hand enquiry and I hoped the children's heightened descriptive language

Figure 1.4 'Behind bars'

would enable them to communicate their observations. Durbin, Morris and Wilkinson firmly believe that artefacts can stimulate great interest:

> Objects have a remarkable capacity to motivate. They develop the 'need to know' which will first spark children's interest, then their curiosity or creativity, and then stimulate their research. Handling objects is a form of active learning that engages children in a way that other methods often fail to do. Objects provide a concrete experience that aids or illuminates abstract thought.
>
> (Durbin *et al*. 1990: 4)

Initially the children did explore the artefacts and asked questions about them. They compared them to the present-day equivalent and learnt a great deal from this activity. To incorporate these artefacts into the role play situation I explained to the children that people couldn't travel a long way to report their stolen property in the olden days. They had to describe it to the local policeman who would then travel on horseback to see if their property had been handed in to the police station. From this further stimulus I observed the children's play and recorded language that was interesting. The following conversation was overheard shortly afterwards:

Child E: Peeler, the baddies have taken my money. It's those big pennies. I need those pennies, are they in your police station?
Child F: Did they take them from your house? What do they look like?
Child G: They are big and there is one that is smooth. They feel heavy, very heavy.

Another child reported her loss to me and said:

Child H: Robbers have taken my pot, the one for the butter.
Teacher: Oh no, I wonder what it was made of?
Child H: Well it was china and was brown. It has a lid that comes off and inside is a thing with holes in it.
Teacher: I wonder how you will keep your butter from melting when it is a hot day.
Child H: I'll have to get it back because they didn't have fridges then, did they?

To me these children had made strides in the use of their descriptive language and the role play area provided the perfect context for exploring objects from the past. They were highly motivated to talk about them and the language revealed a growing knowledge of the past beyond living memory.

Above everything, I felt that this project had given the children an experience that portrayed history as an exciting subject. The children brought their parents to see the police station and in this way involved them with their learning. At the end of the topic, I asked the children what they had learned about Peel and about life long ago. One child summed up his learning as follows:

> Peel was the first man to start the police. He wanted to have a job. The 'Charlies' were before him. The 'Charlies' were the police before him. He fell off a horse. He has died now. Then they built a Peel Tower and then they built a statue of Peel.

Not only was this child's knowledge factually correct, he had sequenced events, used the past tense and used vocabulary related to the passing of time: 'first', 'before', 'now', 'then', 'and then'. I thought this was quite an achievement for a child of just five years of age. Another child stated:

> Long ago they had horses and carriages. They had top hats, truncheons, handcuffs. They blew a whistle very hard because there were no telephones.

This child was showing historical knowledge by explaining why the whistle was blown. My last example remembered some different facts when he said, 'Peel started the police force and let the children out of underground. He didn't want children under eleven to work.'

I felt the children's understanding was partly attributable to the high amount of oral work both in and out of the role play area. History can be an abstract subject for children, who live very much in the concrete 'here and now'. I agree with Williamson and Silvern (1991: 79) when they say: 'Young children whose thinking is still preoperational in nature need direct active experience with phenomena in order to construct schemes for dealing with such phenomena.'

The activities employed complementary programmes of study in both history and English and satisfactory progress was made in both subjects. Although preparation for this project took considerable time this was out-weighed by its cross-curricular nature, satisfying learning objectives in more than one subject.

The role play area was certainly beneficial in maintaining the children's interest in the subject and enabled the artefacts to be used in a meaningful context. The project about Peel started off as a very local study but gave children an insight into Victorian life nationally. Issues concerning child labour and crime at that time are evidence of this. In this way local history links with national history. The understanding the children acquired was directly linked to the opportunity the role play provided for language development in a meaningful context.

Wells sums up the feelings I have about the teaching of oracy in conjunction with other subjects and particularly with history when he states:

> Talking to learn is just as important as reading and writing to learn and we ought to plan so that both are given equal value as complementary modes of thinking and communicating in all areas of the curriculum.
>
> (Wells 1986: 146)

By 'talking to learn', I believe that this role play activity promoted both historical understanding and skills fundamental to the development of literacy.

References

Christie, J. (1991) *Play and Early Literacy Development*, Albany, NY: State University of New York Press.

Durbin, G., Morris, S. and Wilkinson, S. (1990) *A Teacher's Guide to Learning from Objects*, London: English Heritage.

Goodman, K.S. (1982) *Language and Literacy: The Selected Writings of Kenneth S. Goodman*, ed. F.V. Gollasch, London: Routledge and Kegan Paul.

Halliday, M.A.K. (1997) *Learning How to Mean*, New York: Elsevier – North-Holland.

Smith, F. (1978) *Reading*, 2nd edn, Cambridge: Cambridge University Press.

Wells, G. (1986) *The Meaning Makers: Children Learning Language and Using Language to Learn*, London: Hodder and Stoughton.

Williamson, P. and Silvern, S. (1991) 'Thematic Fantasy Play and Story Comprehension', in J. Christie (ed.), *Play and Early Literacy Development*, Albany, N.Y.: State University of New York Press.

2

TALKING ABOUT ARTEFACTS AT KEY STAGE 1

Promoting and assessing listening and speaking

Patricia Nulty

This chapter concerns the ways in which speaking and listening skills can be developed by investigating historical objects. I hope to show that they provide meaningful contexts in which debating skills can be practised. They are particularly useful in enhancing problem-solving skills, which are important in all subjects of the curriculum. In English, problem-solving is necessary when writing narrative or information text; in reading, when analysing; but particularly in discussion, when formulating questions, building up hypotheses and concluding a successful argument are vital. Historical objects also provide activities which enable description skills to be promoted. If the activities are taped, assessment opportunities are also available.

In a Key Stage 1 classroom, artefacts can be introduced as part of an area of study such as 'Famous People' or 'Victorians' (DfE 1995b). They will fulfil the 'Interpretations' and 'Historical Enquiry' aspects of the programmes of study. They will also help children to 'identify differences between ways of life at different times' (2c) and help them 'communicate their awareness and understanding' (5a). An awareness of 'why people did things' (2b) can also be developed.

This chapter considers children's responses to a variety of artefacts, related to the history unit 'Famous People'. In an attempt to counterbalance a western, non-female bias, the people included Cleopatra, Muhammad, Sitting Bull, Mary Seacole, Pochahontas and Elizabeth I. Eight twenty-minute sessions were held with randomly selected year 1 and year 2 children when the class was in assembly, and the discussions were taped. The objects used included Native American jewellery, Egyptian jewellery and plate, Arab clothes, an oil lamp, a steel drum, an eyeletter, a churn and pan-pipes.

Problem-solving and debate

Many authors have seen the use of primary historical material as essential for reasoning and deductive argument (Cooper 1992; Fleming 1982; Smith and Holden 1994; Durbin 1989, 1992; Cowan 1982; Blyth 1995). Like Knight (see Farmer and Knight 1995: 26), I believe that children's reasoning in history is, 'barely different from their logical thinking in general'.

In English, problem-solving is used in argument and discussion. In order to have a discussion, children need a strange object in front of them which they can discuss. Questions tumble out, concerning who owned it, its age, value and use. Observations are made and evidence obtained. Hypotheses are quickly offered and investigated using senses, measurements, tests or through reasoning.

Having an object revealed to them is a motivating experience. By being allowed to handle this precious piece of history, the children will feel empowered. The atmosphere will encourage them to contribute and they will soon realise that there is no 'correct' answer. All that is required is an idea which can be supported. At first, it may be necessary for the adults to ask the questions, if only to model how to interrogate a source. The children will quickly imitate. In my study with random groups of year 1 and year 2 children, they asked questions for information (important for imagination development): 'Is that a lump?' (year 1, when discussing the Egyptians' use of wax); 'Do you think they washed it in a bucket of water?' (year 2).

The year 2 children asked thirty-three questions as part of the group problem-solving situation, aiming them at anyone in the group. Sometimes it seemed as though the children were asking themselves the questions – thinking aloud. Investigating an historical object also allows children to hear many more questions being asked than in a normal class lesson. In seven discussion sessions with the year 1 children, I asked 202 questions and with year 2, 156. Many of my questions were of the clarification type: 'Is that what you mean?'; or trying to involve children who were being a little reticent: 'What do you think?' Later, my questions were noticeably more general: 'Would you tell us about it, please?' Often they would end a series of statements which had summarised their argument to that point.

Having suggested questions, the children went on to hypothesise, test, conclude and support the conclusions. The year 1 group produced a total of 141 hypotheses, while 148 hypotheses were produced by the year 2 group. Six sessions resulted in year 2 testing their hypotheses and four for year 1, such as the following extract of conversation about the Egyptian plate:

R: I think it's a queen and a maid giving her something.
Teacher: Giving her something?
K/A: That might be a King and Queen.
G: Because Kings and Queens have crowns on their heads.
Teacher: They do. So you think they may be crowns then?

General: Yeah.
G: That one's not got a crown.
A: It has!
K: It has but it's different. *(Compares the source sheet)*
B: But there's only one of them sitting on a throne.

English in the National Curriculum (DfE 1995a) requires that children in Key Stage 1 have opportunities to develop, explore and clarify ideas, discuss possibilities, describe observations, give reasons for opinions and actions. They have to work in groups of different sizes and be taught to listen carefully, to ask and answer questions, make relevant comments and remember specific points and consider others' views. They should be taught the importance of clear, fluent and interesting language and they should be able to organise what they have to say, distinguishing between the essential and the inessential. They should also be taught the conventions of discussion and conversation.

Activities involving objects can develop debating skills. They can encourage discussing each others' questions and hypotheses. They involve: listening to their own and others' reasoning; putting forward their own opinions; considering other points of view and testing inferences from evidence in impromptu situations (Cooper 1992: 8). Children can practise making their language effective; considering the audience and the point they are trying to make: all quick-fired decision-making in a discussion situation. They are also given the chance to exercise their 'probability' words and practise their verbal argument skills. Cooper (ibid.: 20) calls for activities which provide 'a means for open and animated thought so that the child has intellectual autonomy, can take risks, exchange ideas and organise thought relative to the thought of others'. Object-based tasks will provide these.

In Cooper's study of led and unled discussion of historical evidence with all types of Key Stage 2 children she found they showed the children's ability to listen to others' points of view and to follow them up with either a further argument or a fresh point. Smith and Holden (1994: 6–9) discovered that using artefacts in group situations encouraged 'purposeful interaction'. To begin with, they made 'tentative guesses'; these then led to 'informed possibilities, using, relating and sharing their own knowledge and understanding'. Brzezicki's (1991: 12–16) investigation with Key Stage 3 children followed similar stages: random unlinked statements which led through discussion to consensus and synthesis. Examples of children's debating techniques are in the section on 'assessment' below.

Description

Describing objects can encourage the development of a broad vocabulary, which can have cross-curricular benefits. Greenfield and Reich (1996: 290) would go further: 'A rich and hierarchically organised vocabulary as well as the syntactical embedding of labels become necessary when one must communicate out of the context of immediate reference.' In such 'labelling' activities, Sonstroem (1966) found that enactive, iconic and symbolic levels of linguistic development were used. In providing describing activities, the pupils' linguistic-symbolic processes are aroused and their 'encoding potential' expanded: 'shortest', 'widest', 'the most spread out'. She found that labelling required manipulation, and vice versa. They interact. These types of activities give children the experience to use many varied descriptive words in many different ways.

Fleming (1982: 165–73) has suggested a concise and orderly framework of description which could include the object's height, weight, colour, shape, material and construction. Objects present a special opportunity for description because of their uniqueness and the mystery surrounding them. Christie (1990) argues that a change in written and spoken language will result from using direct and challenging experiences. Acquiring the techniques of description in such stimulating circumstances will encourage pupils in other areas of the curriculum. Indeed, Richmond (1990: 81) writes, 'The essential business of the language and English curriculum is, in fact, to compose, communicate and comprehend meanings – their own and other people's – in purposeful contexts.'

Assessment

Assessing children's abilities in speaking and listening at the end of Key Stage 1 can be very worrying! How do we give children an equal chance to practise their skills? How can we monitor them fairly? What do we do about the non-speakers? As can be seen above, sessions with objects will provide a class teacher with a considerable amount of evidence on a child's ability to listen and speak.

The National Curriculum document requires that the pupils talk and listen confidently; explore and communicate ideas; show they have listened carefully by making relevant comments and be aware of standard English (DfE 1995a, level 3). In my study, all the year 1 members contributed relevant remarks. Two year 1 children were non-speakers in a full class setting. Possibly in a small group, they felt secure. Another year 1 child was the 'class comedian' and used class discussions as a forum for his wit. The smaller audience encouraged him to make penetrating remarks and revealed much about his ability which was not normally evident due to poor literacy skills.

In talking about an Egyptian plate, for example, it was he who suggested smelling it; he recognised it wasn't new because it had 'dints' in it; he already knew about Cleopatra; he noticed the thick glaze; he suggested an alternative use as a shield and proposed comparing it with the Indian patterns we had been studying.

Improving grammar by rooting it in 'meaningful contexts' (Cox 1984) can also be found in some of our discussions:

G: Them two circles are different.
Teacher: Yes, those two circles are different.

From year 2 there were no other grammatical errors apart from the ubiquitous and sometimes indistinct 'must ov'. Because of the nature of the subject matter, that is, talking about things happening in the past, the phrases 'must have', 'might have', 'could have', 'would have' occurred very frequently and by the end of the course 'have' was clearly in place. As I write twelve months later, however, I realise that this is no longer so and that 'ov' is back, possibly indicating that continuous experience is necessary.

Investigating objects will reveal how children explore and communicate their ideas:

G: I know how they made that.
Teacher: Go on then G.
G: By metal.
Teacher: What have they done to the tin?
K: They've cut the bottom off . . .
G: And knocked it with a hammer.
K: It used to be flat then someone pushed it up . . . to make it round.
Teacher: What are they trying to make?
R: A drum . . .
K: It feels bobbly.
G: They've scratched it.
Teacher: I think they've done more than that – K was very close.
J: Hammered!
Teacher: What do you notice about the bumps?
Ry: Some are bigger (*tapping with a pencil*). It changes to different ones!
                                                              (Steel drum)

This extract also indicates that the children were listening carefully and shows the 'cut and thrust' of their arguments while they are organising their thoughts.

They express their ideas, usually supporting their point of view within the same sentence. They confidently use the language of problem solving: 'I think', 'It might be', 'Maybe', 'Perhaps', 'If you could . . . then you . . .', 'I wonder', 'because', 'looks like', 'could be'. Although these phrases sound tentative they are used to introduce ideas and opinions. Perhaps they act as internal questions which are answered immediately as they speak.

The discussions also prove the maturity of their descriptive powers and vocabulary. For level 3 in 'Listening and Speaking', children are required to 'vary their use of vocabulary and the level of detail':

K: It's got to be a necklace. It's got beads on it and string. It stretches. They are all different colours . . . Little beads . . . straight on one side – three on one side, three on the other . . . made out of something hard . . . picture of a bird . . . An arrow! . . . [It's like a] shield.

(Native American necklace)

A: It's got some holes; a pattern; lumpy bits in the side; a line beside each hole going up the middle . . .

(Eyeletter)

Ry: They're very nice, because in the first place when I saw it I thought they were squares, but they're not – they're diamonds – it's a handle to carry it – it's rough!

(Steel drum)

G: It looks like a necklace . . . It's got lots of beads . . . One side is the same as the other . . . [made of] plastic . . . Maybe they're flowers . . . I don't think it's glass – it's not breaking.

(Native American necklace)

A range of colours was used for the descriptions, for example, silver, gold, green, black, navy blue, grey, bronze, peach, orange, copper (Egyptian plate); green, yellow, black, white, orange, red, blue, pale blue, dark blue (Native American necklace).

The language of shape, size and symmetry was also used. In the conversations, these terms were used quite naturally and often gave us the contexts for clarifying terms. C used: 'not facing the same way'; 'the fat ones are fatter at the top'; 'the thin ones are smaller circles'; 'like a tube'; 'diamonds'. His understanding of symmetry was revealed here:

C: You could just get it, turn it that way and it would be the same . . . if it goes that way it looks like a square and like that, like a rectangle.

(Pan-pipes)

G used the following: circles, rectangle, tubes, triangle; 'They've rolled it over in patterns'. One side is the same as the other. This has a round piece like a snail's back.

(Arab belt)

Ja spoke about 'symmetrical patterns', 'cylinder at the bottom', 'circles', 'pyramid' and 'lower down'. It is perhaps worth quoting part of our discussion on the eyeletter:

Teacher: Does anyone want to tell us about the shape of it?

25

Ja: A cylinder.
Teacher: Yes, these are. So we have different sizes of cylinders on the end of what?
C: The sides are cones.
K: And this is a cuboid.
Teacher: Yes. These are cones on what?
Ca: On like bumpy things.
Ja: Like a sphere.

In my study, year 2 children could also talk and listen with confidence. Table 2.1 shows the number of relevant remarks which would be taken into consideration if they were being assessed for level 3 in 'Speaking and Listening'.

R attempted to dominate the group. As can be seen from the table, her contributions improved over the study. Possibly she felt protected in a small group and this enabled her to have more self-confidence and motivation to contribute properly and listen to the views of others. Trying to solve a common problem which the object presented also tended to lead to a sense of camaraderie and team spirit. There was also a non-speaker in the year 2 group. Over the period of our study, her contributions increased three-fold. The discussions also revealed the way she thought and her knowledge about historical periods:

Cha: Yes, you can feel the dints . . . Yes, but that's been painted on . . .

These remarks drew the attention of the group to how the decoration had been applied to the Egyptian plate:

Cha: There are little gaps there and they're bigger in some places so it can't be new.

While investigating the churn, it was she who hypothesised how liquids could be brought out of the container. In the same discussion, it was she

Table 2.1 The number of children's remarks assessed at level 3, 'Speaking and Listening'

Child	Plate	Jewellery	Clothes	Eyeletter	Necklace	Churn	Pipes
Jo	21	21	8	21	16	20	2
Ch	20	20	15	12	15	27	11
J	15	15	13	12	11	8	23
R	2	2	20	abs	14	22	18
Cha	5	5	8	11	6	13	16
H	1	9	9	12	5	7	4

who made the connection that where the paint had come off on the covered jug was just where the rust had invaded. Since taking part in the study, she occasionally contributes to class discussions. The sessions must have increased her confidence either because she realised her remarks had equal or more value than those of other members and/or because she could not be wrong as long as she supported her views.

The extra experience in discussions may have developed the children's skills so much that they were considered for level 4. For the children to be able to satisfy the criteria for level 4 of the 'Listening and Speaking' elements in English they have to:

> talk and listen with confidence in an increasing range of contexts. Their talk is adapted to the purpose: developing ideas thoughtfully, describing events and conveying their opinions clearly. In discussion, they listen carefully, making contributions and asking questions that are responsive to others' ideas and views. They use appropriately some of the features of standard English vocabulary and grammar.
>
> (DfE 1995a: 18)

Several categories of talk emerged:

Talk adapted to purpose

Jo   The colours are different; the colours are dark and bright. It's shiny. It's tin as well.

(Egyptian plate)

Ch: I think it might have been a plate – a very expensive plate – for a Queen or King.

(Egyptian plate)

J: I think that necklace is for children because I don't think an adult would fit in that.

(Native American necklace)

Ra: I think it's wood because it's been carved – see the pattern there.

(Pan-pipes)

Cha: If it wasn't gold, it might have been paint.

(Egyptian jewellery)

H: This kind of looks like a face. There's the head.

(Egyptian jewellery)

In these extracts each child has recognised what was required in the context, that is, giving their ideas, and, where possible, supporting them.

Developing ideas thoughtfully

Jo: They've been drawn by someone who lived a long time ago because that's how chairs used to be — a little foot there and a stand down there.

(Egyptian plate)

Ch: They might have had a little small cotton reel and put a hole there then this would have gone through the hole and snapped onto the cotton reels.

(Eyeletter)

J: I don't really think it would be good for its job . . . All the milk would get dirty . . . the milk would come out [of the holes] . . . how would you get the milk in? Take the top off?

(Churn)

R: [You must blow it] this end — it's the same shape as my recorder and it's the shape of the lip . . . it's different though — those holes are up there and there's none down here . . . no, there's no note underneath.

(Pan-pipes)

Cha: Those are the same . . . That's got a bump on the edge [scrapes] ooh like a guiro! . . . That could be two instruments . . . You do that — scrape and then blow it . . . Yes it could be two instruments.

(Pan-pipes)

H: It's round, made of wool, soft like wool . . . It's got a knot at the end. Big woolly bits . . . It might be a brownie something underneath . . . It could be a thin piece of wood . . . It's a belt!

(Arab belt)

Describing

Jo: These look like flowers, blossom, at the bottom . . . And there's like a rainbow, [and a triangle]; a box which hasn't got a top, with three ends and it's got white and black all around it and yellow arms.

(Native American necklace)

Ch: Gold . . . Yes it does look greeny gold . . . It changes in the light! It's got white in . . . And it's very padded there. And that chair looks as if it's got a pad underneath it . . . It smells like copper . . . This bit's been

Figure 2.1 Churn

scratched and that's been painted. This bit's got scratched and this bit's newer than that one . . .

(Egyptian plate)

J: It's a necklace and it's got colourful beads on it and a dangling bit . . . And that's a kind of diamond . . . That looks like a bit of wax there.

(Native American necklace)

R: It's orangy . . . It's a peachy colour . . . It smells like it's made out of metal . . .

(Egyptian plate)

It's like shoelaces and wool . . . Cotton and softer, silk . . .

(Arab head-dress)

There's a tiny bit of a pattern . . . See here it's red, white, red, white . . . And that's an arrow shape.

(Native American necklace)

29

H: You press those together in a piece of paper and it makes a hole.

(Eyeletter)

It's silvery brown. It's got some words on it . . .

(Steel drum)

It's too tight . . . I think it's knitted . . . It looks like a robot . . .

(Arab belt)

Cha: . . . diamond. I looked at the pattern to see if it's an Egyptian pattern . . . Well, the pattern's gone round. That's a triangle and that's a triangle . . . Metal . . . Silvery and brown . . . It's a sort of triangular shape on the top . . .

(Egyptian plate)

They used a wide range of terms to describe colour and the discussions were also an excellent vehicle for learning and assessing the language of shape and size.

Using problem-solving language

(Numbers refer to total number of references during the study.)

Jo: I think (20) I know (5) might (6) could (3) If . . . how (2) as . . . if because (6) I wonder would (9) If . . . then.

Cha: I thought (2) I think (7) I know (3) It might (3) Because (2) would (5) perhaps (2) If . . . then (2) how probably (3).

J: If . . . then (3) may have (2) might (4) could have (3) I think (11) could be (2) first . . . then . . . so because (3) perhaps would (2) how.

Ra: Because (4) might (2) I think (3) maybe how could (4) I know.

H: I think (5) I know why might (3) perhaps.

Cha: Might (9) could be (4) would have (2) because I think instead if . . . then.

The tentative 'mights' from Cha contrast with the bold 'I know' from Jo and 'I think' from Ch, Ra, H, Jo, but they speedily decreased over the period, until there were none in the last session.

Responding to each other's ideas and conveying their opinions

Jo: And they've smudgy – fingermarks.

J: They might have just clipped the top on – the bottom bit has not got that bit on.

Teacher: So you're thinking that's a join? Oh, I think you might be right.

Cha: Yes, you can feel it.

J: Yes, they could've smudged the finger marks into the *first* layer of it, then put this bit on.

Ch: Yes, you can actually see the fingermarks. It looks like someone has been naughty and pressed their fingers in when it was wet.

(Egyptian plate)

H: I think it's a spirit.

(Jewellery)

Cha: It looks a bit like a necklace.
Ra: But that's too long for me.
H: You might trip up!
Cha: You'd have to be very tall. It might be for cattle and things if it was for a show.

(Arab head-dress)

Children of this age are unlikely to have vocabularies which are wide enough to convince through language. They are confident enough, however, to use gesture, emphasis and volume. In the quotations above, I have tried to convey these last two using italics and exclamation marks. Usually they try to persuade by argument and reasoning. The children have been quoted exemplifying these characteristics. Sometimes they used experience or knowledge drawn from other sources to try to prove their point, for example, Jo cites videos and his dad as sources; H cites museums as her sources.

It would be very unusual for a teacher to assess a year 2 child as level 4 in any subject but, as can be seen from these extracts, they fulfil the criteria. It may be that their experiences in discussions on tape have helped their confidence and encouraged them to take risks as well as providing contexts for thinking, concentrating and organising their thoughts. As a minimum, the tapes provide evidence that children of this age can achieve these levels and this should make us question whether our expectations are too low.

Tests to evaluate significant differences

The taped discussions had already provided evidence of how historical objects could aid debate and description skills, as well as providing contexts for assessment and problem-solving skills. However, I also wanted to discover how the random groups compared with the rest of the class: that is, if they had progressed more, especially where problem solving and descriptive skills were involved.

I devised a 'test' to discover whether the random groups (T groups) were better able to formulate questions which would lead to hypotheses and subsequently to investigations. The results seem to suggest that year 2 children in the T group were better able to frame questions. They could also go beyond this and were able to think of ways of answering them. Other year 1 children framed more questions than their peers but they were not of the same quality and took a long time to extract. There was a small amount of evidence to suggest that the T group had more idea about how to solve the problem they had posed.

Behaviour during two other class experiments revealed that the T children:

- provided more ideas as to how to proceed;
- provided more hypotheses which could be tested;
- observed events better;
- provided explanations (see Nulty 1997);
- showed more ability in setting up their own experiments.

Had the extra experience of discussion heightened their logical thinking, aroused their potential to imagine and manipulate events outside the immediate and increased their ability to communicate their own and understand others' meanings?

Another 'test' I imposed on all children involved describing an object for someone else to draw. I hoped to compare T groups and other children in the quality of their descriptions and their interpretations. I gave the children a bakelite pot. As well as having a lid, it had an internal pot with a mesh cover. It was originally used for face powder. I divided the children into four groups – two T groups and two other groups. One person out of each group described the object while the others attempted to draw it, unseen.

The drawings of the T groups were better than other groups. Was this because the descriptions were more detailed? In year 1 the T groups' drawings were more recognisable than the others. The decorations were more detailed and appropriate to the descriptions:

R (T group): It's got . . . a round lid . . . on the edge it's got a rumply bit . . . Inside it's got like the top but it is just black and on the lid where it is smoother there is a little line and another little line and on the bottom it has got a round circle and two lines coming from the middle with a round thin circle at the bottom. It has a round shape like a squashed cylinder. It has a flat bottom . . . First the white lid goes on, then the black lid then you have like a cup-cake and it has something like a bag on the white lid . . .

K (T group): It's round with square bits out of it . . . like bubbles . . . two more bobbly bits . . . It's got a round circle under it with writing on and then two straight lines and . . . a round circle with two long bits joined and it's got a lid on it. You can't see it . . . The lid has some white dots on it . . . On the top it's not smooth, its bumpy.

Ma (NT group): It's round . . . It's got a black top. The top turns and it comes off . . . then under the top there's this white thing.

32

Then there's this little container. It looks like a cup but it hasn't got a handle. On the bottom, it's a line, then a circle, then a line . . .

Char (NT group): It's round . . . It's white and there's two rings on the top . . . on top . . . it goes from there to there.

Ma's description is accurate. The other members of his group seem unable to interpret or imagine what he means. Char's group, on the other hand, has no real chance of drawing the correct object because her description is so inaccurate. R and K, however, describe well; four members draw significant features, C's being accurate and recognisable. This seems to indicate that the T group's ability to describe an image is more advanced than that of the children who had not been involved in the artefact sessions.

Conclusion

Historical objects can provide suitable items for exercising descriptive skills. Children practise using verbs, adjectives, shape and material vocabulary and imagination in visualising how they would be used. They also have the opportunity to listen to them being used. The T group children were better able to convey their descriptions and interpret others'. This seems to prove that regular experience in describing objects in purposeful contexts before a small audience promotes descriptive skills, particularly since similar results were found during maths activities and science investigations (see Nulty 1997). Possibly, extra experience in discussions had boosted their interest and confidence in similar situations.

Perhaps they realised their ideas were worthwhile and wished to share them. Perhaps they had been given the listening and speaking skills necessary to participate. Perhaps the T group children had experienced enough discussion around problems to realise that once an idea had been proved wrong, another question had to be raised and tested. Also, they had been given many experiences in realising that there is rarely only one correct answer and that they needed to collect evidence to use as support for opinions.

Assessment possibilities in listening and speaking are readily available in discussion around historical objects. Obviously the choice of object would depend on which area of the curriculum or which topic was being taught. They appear to be particularly useful where 'quiet', unconfident children or those with few literacy skills are concerned. A secure, small group setting gives confidence to these children while the interest surrounding the objects motivates them to share their ideas. Taping the discussions reveals the children's potential, provides evidence of their ability and makes them feel important. I hope to have demonstrated through this new evidence the capabilities of Key Stage 1 children to listen, speak and reason during activities involving historical objects.

References

Blyth, J. (1995) *History 5 to 11*, London: Hodder and Stoughton.

Brzezicki, K. (1991) 'Talking about History: Group Work in the Classroom. Practice and Implications', *Teaching History*, 64: 12–16.

Christie, F. (1990) 'Young Children's Writing: From Spoken to Written Genre', in R. Carter (ed.), *Knowledge about Language and the Curriculum*, London: Hodder and Stoughton.

Cooper, H. (1992) *The Teaching of History*, London: David Fulton.

Cowan, R. (1982) 'The Industrial Revolution in the Home: Household Technology and Social Change in the Twentieth Century', in J. Schlereth (ed.), *Material Culture Studies in America*, New York: American Association for State and Local History.

Cox, B. (1984) *English 5–13*, London: HMSO.

Department for Education (DfE) (1995a) *English in the National Curriculum*, London: HMSO.

Department for Education (DfE) (1995b) *History in the National Curriculum*, London: HMSO.

Durbin, G. (1989) 'Evaluating Learning from Historical Objects', in E. Hooper-Greenhill (ed.), *Initiatives in Museum Education*, Leicester University of Leicester Press.

Durbin, G. (1992) 'History from Objects', in G. Durbin, S. Morris and S. Wilkinson (eds), *A Teacher's Guide to Learning from Objects*, London: English Heritage.

Farmer, A. and Knight, P. (1995) *Active History in Key Stages 3 and 4*, London: Fulton.

Fleming, E. M. (1982) 'Artefact Study: a Proposed Model', in J. Schlereth (ed.), *Material Culture Studies in America*, New York: American Association for State and Local History.

Greenfield, P. and Reich, L. (1966) 'On Culture and Equivalence', in J. Bruner, R. Olver and P. Greenfield (eds), *Studies in Cognitive Growth*, New York: John Wiley.

Jones, M.F. and Madeley, R. (1983) *Using Objects to Learn: Visual Awareness and Language Development in the Classroom*, Ontario: Royal Ontario Museum.

Nulty, P. (1997) 'Working with Historical Objects in an Interdisciplinary Context: a Case Study at KS1, unpublished MEd dissertation, University College Chester.

Richmond, J. (1990) 'What Do We Mean by Knowledge about Language?', in R. Carter (ed.), *Knowledge About Language and the Curriculum*, London: Hodder and Stoughton.

Smith, L. and Holden, C. (1994) 'I Thought It Was for Picking Bones Out of Soup', *Teaching History*, 76: 6–9.

Sonstroem, A. (1966) 'The Conservation of Solids', in J. Bruner, R. Olver and P. Greenfield (eds), *Studies in Cognitive Growth*, New York: John Wiley.

3

STORYTELLING IN HISTORY

Alan Farmer and Christine Cooper

History isn't just what happened. History is just what historians tell us ... The history of the world? Just voices echoing in the dark; images that burn for a few centuries and then fade; stories, old stories that sometimes seem to overlap; strange links, impertinent connections. We lie in our hospital bed of the present (what nice clean sheets we get nowadays) with a bubble of daily news drip-fed into our arm. We think we know who we are, though we don't quite know why we're here, or how long we shall be forced to stay. And while we fret and writhe in bandaged uncertainty – are we a voluntary patient? – we fabulate. We make up a story to cover the facts we don't know or can't accept; we keep a few true facts and spin a new story round them. Our panic and our pain are only eased by soothing fabulation; we call it history.

(Barnes 1989: 242)

This is an extract from Julian Barnes's *History of the World in Ten and a Half Chapters*. It should be said at the outset that we do not fully accept the view that history is nothing but story (nor, we suspect, does Barnes). There is rather more to history than simply story. However, we do regard story as a vital element of history at every level. Like Joan Blyth (1982), we see story as 'the essence of history teaching'. In this chapter we are concerned essentially with storytelling. Until the last decade, storytelling in history seemed to be a dying art. One of us was able to write in the 1980s that 'the History storyteller is becoming something of an endangered species' (Farmer 1990). However, something of a resurrection has recently taken place. Many historians, teachers and educationalists now accept that storytelling is still very much at the heart of history teaching – at all levels, but particularly at Key Stages 1 and 2. Story can be read. But stories can also be told. This chapter is concerned with what makes a good history story and storyteller, particularly at Key Stage 2. We have our own views – and also the views expressed by a small sample of (18) primary teachers who attended the

Grants for Education, Support and Training (GEST) history course in 1997 and who completed a questionnaire on story (see Appendix A). Although the sample was small, most of the teachers were curriculum co-ordinators of history and their responses gave us plenty of food for thought. Finally, we have some tips for storytellers and an example of how storytelling might cash out in practice.

The relationship between history and story

Chris Husbands (1996: 46) is right when he says: 'The relationship between history and story has always been a difficult one.' In many European languages story and history are one and the same word (*histoire* in French, *Geschichte* in German, *storia* in Italian) and story is a major component of the English word history. The great British historians, from Bede, through Gibbon and Macaulay, to Churchill, were great storytellers. A.J.P. Taylor, one of the twentieth century's best historians (and storytellers) stated that 'we shouldn't be ashamed to admit that history at bottom is simply a form of storytelling . . . there is no escaping the fact that the original task of the historian is to answer the child's question: "What happened next?"' (Taylor 1983).

However, many historians and teachers have been sceptical about the place of story in the teaching and learning of history. Academic history has often been dismissive of 'mere' story: too much narrative and not enough analysis has long been considered a major crime in history undergraduate essays. Many teachers and educationalists have also been critical of story. From the late 1960s onwards story was associated with what David Sylvester (1994: 9) calls the 'great tradition' of history teaching based upon the teacher relaying mainly British, mainly political history to essentially passive pupils. Storytelling was suspect in the eyes of those who favoured a child-centred approach. The teacher, in this view, is really no longer an authority or even necessarily in authority. Instead, he or she is a facilitator and collaborator in the learning process. Storytelling seemed to be at odds with the 'active' approach. For children actually to sit and listen seemed to go against the 'progressive' grain: emphasis was placed instead on developing classroom methodologies which encouraged children to develop their learning through the active use of language rather than through listening or even writing. (Interestingly, the 1967 Plowden Report, which many associate with 'active' learning, actually commended the use of story, suggesting that children are interested in history because they are interested in stories, many of which are not to be distinguished from literature. Children should not be denied stories like Odysseus, Beowulf and the Norse stories.)

The introduction of so-called 'new history' in the early 1970s was another threat to storytelling. Underpinning the approach of the new history was Bruner's view of the spiral curriculum. Children do what real historians do.

Real historians examine primary sources: therefore children must examine primary sources. Real historians don't tell stories: therefore there was no place for storytelling in school history. By the early 1980s there was a general assumption (among many in the educational establishment at least) that if children were not handling sources they were not doing history; if they were not busy 'doing', they were not learning; if they were not involved in group interaction, something was wrong. Faced with these ideological challenges, storytelling fell into disrepute.

It should be said that critics of story remain. Some fear that stories appear to locate too much power in the hands of the teacher. The storyteller/teacher can oversimplify: can sketch characters as caricatures and complex situations as archetypes of good or evil. Arguably, when the teacher 'takes for granted' the moral basis or outcome of a story or an episode in history, the children learning from it are denied the opportunity critically and democratically to decide their own version or interpretation of what 'this story means or shows' (Bage 1996: 49). Storytellers can impose coherence where there is none. They can promote acceptance, close down possibilities and exclude questioning.

Storytelling and history teaching

However, story and storytelling are now very much back in fashion in education in general and in history teaching in particular. Most history educationalists now agree that story has a powerful appeal for most children and plays an important role in the way they come to understand history and make sense of an often bewildering and confusing past. 'Underlying pupils' thinking . . . seems to be the idea of a past which happens in stories', writes Peter Lee (1991: 54). 'Narratives are an integrative component in historical thinking', asserts Chris Husbands. 'Storied thinking is a central tool in the teaching and learning of history' (Husbands 1996: 51). Hilary Cooper (1995: 50) believes that stories are important in the cognitive development of young children: 'stories affect children's intellectual growth for they do not listen passively; they are called upon to create new worlds through powers of imagination . . . Stories extend first hand experiences of the world . . . so extending perceptions of the world.' Grant Bage (1995), in particular, as well as offering a rationale for the centrality of story in thinking, has examined how the use of spoken stories can make historical narrative richer and more susceptible to analysis by children.

The teacher is the major resource in any classroom: someone who is not just in authority but also an authority. Teachers have a wider frame of historical reference than pupils in selecting the kind of history their pupils will receive. They provide some kind of pattern in an effort to determine the meaning of the past. The way teachers use language in lessons plays a central role in the way that children learn. While teacher talk can give too much away, it need not necessarily do so. Indeed, story should support children's thinking, not replace it: 'The way teachers describe the past is a powerful element in the way pupils construct their own images of the past' (Husbands 1996: 92). Narrative is a crucial way in which young children organise their understanding of the world and the main mode in which they articulate their ideas. Thus its role in the teaching and learning process should not be underestimated.

Storytelling is, and always has been, vitally important with children, possibly those with Special Educational Needs, who have not mastered the skills of reading and writing. But most teachers are also aware that many 'literate' children find that the printed page lacks the sparkle and excitement of a spoken story, which can also be a wonderful shared experience. Story can generate interest and curiosity, conjuring up a picture of the past which is vivid and immediate. It can enrich children's imagination and help them see things from the point of view of people in the past. Story can give an understanding of time. It can also make children want to pursue the tale and thus encourage them to read more about people and events in the past.

Educationalists now generally accept that there is nothing wrong with children being encouraged to listen. The fact that they are sitting quietly does not mean that their brains and imaginations are not hard at work. Alan Bullock and his team stressed the importance of listening in *A Language for Life* (DES 1975), in which they argued that listening can increase a child's ability in the use of language, can influence attitudes, values and conduct, can enrich the imagination, and can encourage a child to read. The notion that children can only listen effectively for a few minutes at a time is something of an old wives' tale and not based on good research evidence or common sense. A child's interest span is just that – an interest span. If the story and storyteller are good enough, children will listen.

Kieran Egan has particularly stressed the importance of story. He has argued that Piaget and many other educational researchers focused too exclusively on a narrow set of logico-mathematical operations and, in so doing, have virtually ignored children's extraordinary ability to fantasise. He points out that the child 'who cannot on the one hand conserve liquid quantity may, on the other, lead a vivid intellectual life, brimming with knights, dragons, witches and star warriors' (Egan 1983: 360). Egan claims that 'children's imaginations are the most powerful and energetic tools', and also believes that the story form is a cultural universal: 'everyone, everywhere, enjoys stories' (Egan 1988: 2). Story is not just some casual entertainment: instead, it reflects a basic and powerful form in which we make sense of the world. This being so, he puts forward a strong case for teachers to adopt both the story form in the planning of their lessons and also storytelling in their teaching method.

Egan's views correspond closely with the views expressed by our surveyed teachers. They suggested that the most common reason for using story in history was to introduce a topic, particularly as it was an efficient vehicle for creating atmosphere and excitement. This was reflected in comments such as: 'I use it to capture children's imagination' and 'Story enables history to come alive'. Other teachers' responses noted the appeal to a child's love of stories and the relevance of narrative to children. One noted the link with English and claimed that the use of story enabled her to 'gain time for history from English'. Indeed, this may be even more necessary with the introduction into primary schools of the 'literacy hour', leaving less time for history than after the Dearing review of the curriculum.

As all teachers of young children know, the listening element of story-telling or reading introduces children to the syntax and semantics which will be fundamental to the children's own reading development. Listening to story provides an introduction to the peculiarities of historical vocabulary. It enables children to become familiar with, and get their tongues round, those words which cause us all to reach for a guide to pronunciation – the Polydectes and Persephones of Ancient Greece and the Quezalcoatls of the Aztecs. Storytelling in the oral tradition is about entertainment. What better entertainment than hearing these new, exotic sounds which not only introduce children to a magically different world but which also enable them to read such complex letter strings?

Increasingly, those teachers who are involved with reception classes have acknowledged that children come to school already equipped with much knowledge about language. Teachers are aware of the richness of such experience and use it as a foundation upon which to build the skills, concepts and attitudes necessary for the child's linguistic development. Similarly, children come to school with a wealth of stories which relate to their personal and family histories, as well as history-based stories gleaned from tapes, books, television and video. Obviously, the depth of experience will depend on the child's circumstances. Howe and Johns (1992: vii) note how some cultural backgrounds reflect the 'story telling community'. They refer to a 'story telling ladder', the lowest rung comprising anecdotes, jokes and family stories and the highest rung involving 'explanations of life and the universe'. On entering school, children will, to a lesser or greater extent, have experienced a variety of anecdotes and family stories, possibly stimulated by photographs, or the chance encounter with music from the past which may result in a grandparent telling the story of 'the day I saw the Rolling Stones'. The odd artefact, such as a flat iron being used as a door-stop, may provide the stimulus for anecdote. By such means children are introduced to ways to investigate the past. This is formalised at Key Stage 1 and develops throughout Key Stage 2 as children realise that older people's stories, written sources and artefacts are means by which they can find answers to their questions about the past.

Finally, we think that there are a large number of stories – local, national and international – which should be part of every child's culture. School

history should fulfil an essentially socialising and integrative role, introducing children to the intellectual and cultural traditions of the society of
which they will become adult members.

What makes a good story?

Storytelling then is, or should be, an essential component of the methodo-
logical armour of history teaching. But what makes a good history story?
First of all, what actually constitutes a history story? Aristotle said that a
story has a beginning which sets up expectations, a middle – or muddle – that
complicates them, and an end that satisfies them. Arguably this definition is
a bit too restrictive. Many of the best history stories are essentially anecdotal.
These anecdotes are not stories by Aristotle's definition; but they are the stuff
of good history. We think that any teacher talk about the past which holds the
children's imagination, whether about gladiators in a Roman amphitheatre or
about life on the home front in the Second World War, are essentially stories,
albeit that the teacher is talking not about specific individuals but about how
masses of people in the past used to live.

That said, there are classic Aristotelian stories, especially in the Greek,
Egyptian, Roman, Saxon, Viking and Tudor units. In our view the best 'pure'
history stories for children have a relatively simple plot and just one or two
central characters. Too much clutter and too many irrelevancies affect the
rhythm of the story. Classic stories (like Boudicca, 1066 and all that, the
Spanish Armada, the Gunpowder Plot – which we hope you still teach
despite the demise of the Stuarts!) need a good start that captures the
imagination and a good end which pulls together all the threads of the plot.

Kieran Egan, in a number of books and articles, has stressed that children
at different ages need stories to be delivered in different ways. He suggests
that most children between the ages of about five to eight are at the 'mythic'
stage of development. He claimed that they think in ways redolent of the
old myth-stories which are built on the conflict of binary opposites. Egan
suggests that after the 'mythic' stage children move on to the 'romantic'
stage. Egan argues he is not putting forward a new stage theory. He sees
children as accumulating layers one on top of another, the new layers inter-
facing and coalescing with parts of the old layer. But he does see a major
difference in the way most children think, and see the world, before and after
eight or nine. At the 'mythic' stage most children readily accept magic or
fantastic elements. They are unperturbed by the process whereby Cinderella's
Fairy Godmother suddenly appears and turns mice into footmen and a
pumpkin into a coach. Most children aged eight upwards will not accept
this. Their stories require internal consistencies and more reality. 'History
is best understood at this [romantic] stage as a kind of mosaic of bright
elements – anecdotes, facts, dramatic events – which are composed into a
small story which in turn is a segment of a larger story' (Egan 1979: 45). He

believes that the quality of heroism is a particularly effective catcher of children's imagination and claims that 'heroizing is a condition of making the world and experience meaningful to middle-school students' (Egan 1990: 127). He stresses that this does not mean that children should necessarily be fed a diet of traditional heroes and heroines which might reinforce forms of submissive class consciousness or sexual stereotyping. But he points out that heroic qualities can be found in anything. We can reflect quite different values by our choice of quite different people. Romantic heroising might be value-laden but this cannot be avoided: what we cannot do – and also hope to educate – is represent no values.

Egan goes on to claim that most children between eight and fifteen are 'fascinated by the extreme, the bizarre, the wonderful' (Egan 1978: 21). Teachers need to stimulate a sense of awe, wonder and even horror. The more alien the world with which students can be connected, the more relevant might the knowledge about it be to their educational development. This may be going too far. But Egan is surely right when he stresses that history lessons should be full of the most exotic and odd societies and people and emphasise dramatic personalities and events. The best history stories are often about bizarre events and improbable people doing the oddest things. The more remote from everyday life, the more macabre, the more 'blood and gore', the better! This love of the gory, erotic and bizarre, claims Egan, is not some immature defect that should be repressed: rather, it is a reflection of the profound truth that only when boundaries are known can one meaningfully chart details within them.

Egan offers a cogent and persuasive description of children's historical interests. It is a pity that so much recent debate on the history teaching front has ignored his theories. There is general acceptance among teachers that good gory incident can sustain flagging attention and ensure that pupils pay some attention to more important but less intrinsically interesting matters. Henry VIII's wives are far more interesting to most children (and adults) than the Reformation. Focusing on the fate of the wives, however, does allow the teacher to explain some of the key points of the Reformation.

A good story needs plenty of action, drama and suspense. Will Boudicca defeat the Romans? Who will win the battle of Hastings? Will the Armada succeed? How will factory and coal mining conditions improve? Will the RAF win the Battle of Britain? Teachers know that the soap opera technique – find out tomorrow/next week what happens next – works well with all aspects of story.

The intrinsic interest of a historical story often lies in its detail. When telling children about the execution of Mary, Queen of Scots, it is essential to describe the scene at Fotheringay Hall on February 1587: the hastily gathered audience; the equally hastily constructed scaffold; Mary's last hours (listening to the scaffold being constructed); her costume and bearing; her last words; how many strokes it took to remove her head; and the embarrassment of the executioner as he held up her wig rather than her severed head. There is, of course, a danger that too much irrelevance can detract from the plot, slow down the action and ruin the story.

One essential aspect, identified by our teacher survey, was that a good story must have clear language. We would add to this the importance of an appropriate style. We have all found authors whose stories – thanks to the choice of relevant language (and content and construction) – never fail to interest children and which 'read' or 'tell' themselves. Our sample of teachers particularly liked stories which presented clear visual images. A good example of this can be found in *The Last Train*, by Kim Lewis (1994: 21):

> James froze. In a thundering hiss of steam, a train blew out of the wind . . . He watched unbelieving, as the train grew bigger and bigger, puffing slower and slower, steam billowing out over the railway line. He saw Sara wave the red handkerchief. Rain hissed down on the hot train, spitting on the metal. . . . The train brakes thundered and squealed.

One advantage of the use of story in history is its ability to create vivid pictures in the child's mind. This is important, especially when illustrations are difficult to come by or, as with some published schemes, are somewhat dull.

In telling the story, teachers should not be disrespectful of the truth. The past once existed. History is not an enterprise in fiction. There is an obligation to be accurate in terms of what can be derived from the historical evidence. The storyteller, however, might put words in the mouths of the characters without there being evidence that the words were actually spoken. The storyteller might also 'invent' historical characters and place them in 'real' historical situations. This, after all, is how historical novelists earn their salt, and good historical novels can be more effective than hard history in helping children understand the past. 'To make a bygone age live again history must not be merely eked out by fiction . . . it must be turned into a good novel' (Husbands 1996: 59). Inherent historical probability is justifiable and potentially highly rewarding.

A good story, by itself, is not enough to make a good storytelling session. The qualities of the storyteller and the nature of the audience are also essential ingredients. The storyteller can interact with a class in a way that is impossible when chained to a book, the text of which can wipe out all natural rhythms and mannerisms. We agree strongly with Jane Wilson's (1979: 38–9) view: 'When a story is shaped and moulded and spoken afresh by a storyteller . . . a living, strong message will come out.' Finding appropriate stories and anecdotes in the first place is time-consuming. It is a life-long process in which teachers acquire their stories in a variety of ways, such as published history schemes, schools' own library resources, stories brought in by the children, and stories acquired in popular adult history books and historical novels. Our surveyed teachers also mentioned the usefulness of schools' broadcasting programmes.

Learning stories is also a slog, like revising for an examination or learning a drama script. Moreover, there is no infallible recipe for success. Good storytellers each have their own idiosyncrasies, styles and qualities. Some use a highly exaggerated and dramatic style: others are soft-voiced and reserved. Rhythm, pitch, clarity, intensity and variety in pace and tone are difficult things to describe, never mind deliver. What is an interesting voice to one person may be boring to someone else. Just as important as the voice is the non-verbal communication aspect: suitable posture, good eye contact and appropriate gestures. A twinkle in the eye usually causes a twinkle in the voice. The main thing is to develop your own style and to have confidence in that style. Faith in the story is essential. If the story appeals to you then it stands a better chance of appealing to the audience. You also need to be involved in the story as you are telling it. This usually entails having a detailed visual picture of it and envisaging it happening as you tell it. Visual aids of all kinds – puppets, pictures, maps, and artefacts – can help the storytellers cause. So can asking questions of the children. There is obviously a need for a degree of empathy with the class – first in the choice of a suitable story and then in reacting to the children's responses. Above all, there is a need for spontaneity. According to Wilson (1979), a story needs to become 'so much a part of yourself that it flows freely'. In this way the story becomes a personal experience: a new creation every time you tell it (Colwell 1980: 41).

Storytelling can be enhanced by the use of a storyteller's hat, staff, cloak or props which enable the teacher to be identified as a neutral agent or as a character from the story. Telling stories in role (for example, Henry VIII giving his version of the 'Break with Rome') can work well. For those who are able to work in pairs (for example, with trainee teachers), it is possible to arrange a grand entrance of the storyteller, in role, possibly in costume or disguise, complete with artefacts (invariably replicas!) relevant to the story. Professional storytellers can be a great source of stimulation and it is not uncommon to find the odd Roman Legionary, Viking or Bomber Pilot holding forth in a classroom. These can provide a welcome alternative for those of us who feel less than comfortable pretending to be Boudicca or Montezuma one minute and explaining the intricacies of percentages the next.

The creation of a storytelling environment, which can involve the use of screens, pictures, rearranged furniture, music and artificial lighting, may seem a massive effort in these days of the overcrowded timetable, but it can transform a history session. We should also point out that readymade storytelling environments exist in the form of sites and buildings. (The use of re-creations and role plays is increasingly becoming a feature of many of our great history sites.) Such environments can be used or created by children in the role of storytellers. (Several surveyed teachers mentioned children being cast in this role.) Preparation for such an activity can form the basis of children's research along the lines of 'Let's find out the background before we create our story'. If appropriate, such stories could be based on artefacts (see Chapter 1). Children can produce storyboards to illustrate the narrative or work on a taped story or video.

There is no storytelling, by teacher or by children, without listeners, and listeners have an active role in any story session. Listeners' reactions, their expressions of excitement, enthusiasm, boredom, apathy or concern, help shape the pace, tone and texture of the story. The best storyteller armed with the best story has to take into account the age, sophistication and interests of the class. Children can inspire or destroy the would-be storyteller. This is as it should be. Storytelling is communal – a constant interaction between the teller and the audience. It is not always necessary to follow up a story with written work, but it can also be an excellent stimulus, providing a way into a topic, providing material for a whole range of investigative and creative follow-up work.

From theory and tips to practice

How might these tips cash out in practice? Let us try and give a concrete example. The career of Alfred the Great provides good storytelling material. With younger pupils Alfred should probably be taught as a good 'thing'/ king, a genuine English hero battling against adversity in the form of the Vikings. Although a mythic version may be a simplification of the truth, it is not necessarily unhistorical. Most serious scholars – Keynes and Lapidge, Stenton, Smyth – consider Alfred 'great'. (One of us is far from certain they are right!) Moreover, the Vikings can clearly be depicted as the baddies. The revisionist attempt to argue that the Vikings were more than rapists, murderers and pillagers and have simply had a bad – Christian – press has some validity but should not conceal the fact that many of the Vikings who came to Britain in the ninth century were rapists, murderers etc.

Alfred's story can be told at one fell swoop. It is even better told over several sessions, permitting teachers to finish at a point that enables them to say: find out next time what happens next. Alfred's story conveniently breaks down into several parts:

849–71 His childhood; the journey to Rome to see the Pope; the winning of the book (a legend); the Viking threat from 865 to 871; the battle of Ashdown; Alfred becomes king in 871; will he and Wessex survive?
871–8 Further problems with the Vikings; the Viking attack on Chippenham in early 878. What should Alfred do now? Flee abroad? Fight? The burning of the cakes (legend); Athelney; the victory at Edington; the

capture of Guthrum. What should Alfred do to Guthrum? Is Alfred now secure?

878–99 Alfred's reforms; his interest in learning; the return of the Vikings; Alfred and Wessex hold out; Alfred's death and legacy. (His son Edward the Elder and grandson Athelstan went on to conquer the Danelaw and bring the whole of England under West Saxon control. They were probably greater than Alfred.)

In Appendix B we have written the bare bones of a story that you might tell to children about the events of 878. By telling the story in your own way, you will certainly improve on it. It needs rather more in the way of detail. It lacks an element of violence. A pity Alfred didn't think of some nasty way of killing Guthrum (for the teacher, that is, not for Guthrum!). But no doubt the children will think of unpleasant things that Alfred might have done to Guthrum. You may have whetted their appetites by telling them that the Vikings are thought to have used King Edmund of East Anglia as target practice for their archers, and there is the Viking saga of King Aella of Northumbria suffering the blood eagle death. But we think the events of 878 provide a tight plot. The story is helped by the fact that there are just two main characters: Alfred (the hero) and Guthrum (the villain). There is plenty of action, drama and suspense. The story even has some humour – with the legendary story of the burning of the cakes.

Having told the story – or indeed while you are telling it – you can introduce children to the sources. How do we know the events in this story happened? The *Anglo-Saxon Chronicle* is the key text. Give year 5 or year 6 pupils the relevant part of the *Chronicle* (which is very short). Bishop Asser's life of Alfred is the only other source but unfortunately this may well be a late tenth-century forgery. It is worth pointing out to older children that the *Anglo-Saxon Chronicle* was compiled at Alfred's court. In other words, we only have a West Saxon version of events. Perhaps, therefore, he was not as great as the story suggests and as most historians think. It is also worth stressing the paucity of the evidence. From little acorns great trees can grow. But is the tree simply foliage? This story, like all stories, should be subject to critical examination. Were the events really like this?

There are a vast range of follow-up activities. Children can be encouraged to shape and order the facts into their own narrative – a vital learning process in both history and English. They might write their own *Chronicle* version of 878. They might do an obituary for Alfred. A 'This is your Life, Alfred the Great' – introduced by Aespel (which sounds a bit Anglo-Saxonish) – can work well. You might get them to tell the story from Guthrum's point of view so that they realise that your story – or any story – is not the definitive version of the tale. Get them to design an Anglo-Saxon or Viking newspaper, or make a radio drama of a scene (with sound effects). The possibilities for artistic or role-play follow-up activities are massive.

Conclusion

In conclusion, this defence of story is not a criticism of other teaching methods. There is a place in history for handling evidence, for 'doing', for group interaction – and for a variety of other activities. But there is also a place for story. Storytelling is one of the vital ways in which teachers can help children understand history. A good story can enrich children's imagination and help them empathise. It can also help children develop their concept of causality. Stories, after all, are about what people did, why they did things and what happened as a result. Stories should raise questions. They should stimulate an interest in history and should encourage further investigation. Not all stories will succeed. But nevertheless story can be one of the most potent ways of explaining to children the events of the past and of transferring your enthusiasm to the class as a whole. Many children enjoy and are fascinated by a good story well told. They have the capacity to transform and create out of what they receive. Most primary teachers have the potential to be good storytellers. Hopefully, storytelling will ensure that many history sessions end as happily ever afterwards as ever happens in real (teaching) life.

Appendix A: possible questions for storytellers

We are attempting to get a picture of how stories are used in history teaching at Key Stage 2. The results will be used as part of a chapter for a new book on teaching history. For the purposes of the study the following would be included in the term 'story': myths, legends, stories based on an event such as the Gunpowder Plot, people, and those which cover 'How we used to live'.

- Why might you use a story in history teaching?
- Which stories have you used?
- What, in your opinion, makes a good history story?
- Please tick any of the following methods which you have used to develop history through storytelling:
  — teacher reading
  — teacher telling
  — teacher telling, in role
  — visiting story tellers
  — children telling stories
  — children reading stories for themselves
  — children reading stories to others
  — use of visual aids
  — use of puppets
  — creation of a storytelling environment
  — use of music.

- Which history study units have you used story for?
- Where have your stories originated from, e.g. library, textbooks, etc.?
- Please tick any activities or follow-up work that have resulted from the use of story:
  — creative writing
  — art work
  — sequencing
  — hot-seating
  — role play
  — freeze-framing
  — creation of newspaper
  — cartoon, or comic strips
  — other – please specify.
- Are there any difficulties which you have found when attempting to teach history through story?

Appendix B: Alfred the Great

Most people have good years and bad years. Sometimes things go well. Sometimes things go badly. Some years are also more important in people's lives than others. The year 878 was certainly an important year for King Alfred the Great. Was it a good year for him or was it a bad year? That is something for you to decide. But first you need to know what happened to Alfred in the year 878.

I think you will know by now that Alfred was King of Wessex. In 878 he had ruled Wessex for nearly seven years. He had spent much of that time fighting against the Vikings. Sometimes he had beaten them. Sometimes they had beaten him. The Vikings were a very dangerous enemy. By the start of the year 878 they had conquered every Anglo-Saxon kingdom – except Alfred's kingdom of Wessex. Many Vikings hoped to conquer Wessex. They would then rule the whole of England. Maybe England – or Angle-land – would then be called Viking-land.

In 878 Alfred was threatened by a Viking army, led by King Guthrum. Alfred gathered his own fighting men at Chippenham. Guthrum and his Vikings were a few miles away. Alfred thought he was safe. Armies at this time didn't usually fight in the winter. It was much nicer to stay indoors and feast in warm halls than march and fight in cold weather.

'It's Christmas,' Alfred told his men. 'Let's enjoy ourselves. The Vikings won't attack us at this time of the year.'

But, unfortunately, Alfred got it wrong. Guthrum and his Vikings believed in the gods Odin and Thor. They weren't Christian and didn't celebrate Christmas. A few days after Christmas, while Alfred and his men were still feasting and drinking, Guthrum attacked Chippenham. Alfred was taken completely by surprise. The Vikings captured Chippenham and quickly took over much of Wessex. Many people thought that Alfred had died in the fighting.

But Alfred was lucky. He managed to escape from Chippenham. With a few loyal followers he fled westwards, away from the Vikings. Even so, this was a bad time for Alfred. He seems to have lost his kingdom and he was still in danger of losing his life.

There is a very famous story about Alfred from this time. One day, according to the story, Alfred got separated from his followers and lost his way in a forest. He wandered through the forest for a while. Then it started to rain. Alfred finally found a lonely swineherd's hut. He knocked on the door and asked for shelter. The swineherd's wife did not recognise him and Alfred did not tell her who he was. After all, he was on the run from the Vikings and didn't want to give himself away. The swineherd's wife said he could shelter from the rain.

'I have many jobs to do,' she said. 'You're not doing much. Can you watch over my bread-cakes which are baking over the fire? Please make sure they don't burn.'

Alfred agreed to keep an eye on the bread-cakes. But his mind was soon on other matters. How would he find his followers? Where should he go? What should he do? How could he beat the Vikings and recover his kingdom? Not surprisingly, Alfred soon forgot all about the bread-cakes. When the swineherd's wife returned to her hut, Alfred was still deep in thought and the bread-cakes were burning.

'You silly man,' she said. 'Look what you've done. My bread-cakes are ruined.'

Just as Alfred was about to apologise, there was a knock on the door and Alfred's followers arrived. Alfred was delighted to see them and they were delighted to find their king. The swineherd's wife now realised that the man she had been scolding was the king! She was very embarrassed. But Alfred didn't mind. After all, it wasn't the woman's fault she hadn't recognised him and she was right to tell him off for burning the cakes.

This is a famous story. Unfortunately it is only a legend. It probably never happened. The story seems to have been made up hundreds of years after Alfred's death.

But we do know that Alfred fled into the treacherous marshlands of Somerset. There, he made his way by secret tracks to the 'isle' of Athelney. Athelney wasn't a proper island. It was just firm land in the middle of wet marshland. But Alfred knew it was a good place to come to.

'It will be hard for the Vikings to find us here,' he told his followers. 'Even if they do find us they will find it difficult to cross the marshes. We will build a fort here. This will be our base. From here we will plan to win back our land from the Vikings.'

Messengers were sent to spread the word that Alfred was still alive.

Throughout the spring and summer the Vikings terrorised Wessex, stealing and killing. But at least the people of Wessex now had some hope.

'Our king is alive,' they whispered. 'One day he will return and drive out the Vikings.'

A few of Alfred's friends thought he should march out and fight the Vikings immediately. But Alfred was more patient.

'We will wait until the summer,' he said. 'Then we will raise a large army and beat the Vikings.'

There is another famous legend about Alfred from this time. This story was first told by a monk called William of Malmesbury in the twelfth century. According to William of Malmesbury:

> While Alfred was in Athelney, he wished to find out the plans of the Viking army. So he disguised himself as a wandering minstrel and juggler and went bravely into the Viking camp. No one suspected who he was and he managed to get right into the middle of the Viking camp. There he overhead the Viking leaders discussing the war. Alfred sat quietly strumming his harp and listened to what they were saying. In this way he found out all the Vikings' secret plans. He stayed in the camp a few more days until he was satisfied that he knew everything. Then he made his way back to Athelney. He gathered all his own leaders. He told them what he had found and how easy it would be to beat the Vikings.

Another nice story! Unfortunately, like the story of Alfred and the cakes, it is only a legend. Most historians think the story was made up by William of Malmesbury. Certainly no one at the time when Alfred was alive wrote anything about it. It seems a bit unlikely that Alfred would have risked his life in this way. After all, someone in the Viking camp might have recognised him. And that would have been the end of Alfred the not-so-great!

By the early summer of 878 Alfred was ready to march against the Vikings. He sent messages to all parts of Wessex.

'Meet me at Egbert's stone in the first week of June,' he told all the fighting men. A large army gathered and Alfred rode from Athelney to join them. 'Now we will get our revenge,' he said. 'We will fight and beat Guthrum and his Vikings.'

He led his men towards a village called Edington. There he fought against the Viking army. There was a great battle. The two sides were evenly matched. Spears flew through the air. Swords clashed against swords. Axes bit into shields and helmets. Both sides fought bravely. Many men died. Many more were wounded. But in the end Alfred and his men were successful and Guthrum and his Vikings fled from the battlefield. Alfred chased the Vikings to their camp at Chippenham. His army surrounded

Chippenham so that no Vikings could get in or out. Soon Guthrum and his men were short of food. They had no choice but to surrender.

What do you think Alfred should have done to Guthrum? The Vikings had killed many people in Wessex and many Saxons had died fighting against them. Some of Alfred's advisers thought the only good Viking was a dead one. They thought Alfred should kill Guthrum and all the Vikings. But Alfred showed mercy. Guthrum was treated well and Alfred tried to make friends with him. The Viking king promised not to attack Wessex again. He also agreed to become Christian. A few days later Guthrum and many of his men were baptised as Christians. Then they returned to those parts of England which they had already conquered.

So was 878 a good year or a bad year for Alfred? By the end of the year 878 Wessex was free of Vikings and Alfred was firmly in control of his kingdom. Moreover, Guthrum seems to have kept his promise. He did not attack Wessex again. But the story does not end happily ever afterwards. (Few stories in real history do!) Alfred had not driven the Vikings out of the whole of England and he had to fight more battles against other Vikings later in his reign. Find out more about this, next week!

Even so I think that on the whole 878 had been a good year for Alfred the Great. What do you think?

References

Bage, G. (1995) 'Chaining the Beast: an Examination of how the Pedagogic Use of Spoken Stories May Make Historical Narrative Richer and More Susceptible to Analysis by Children. An Autobiographical Research Study by an Advisory Teacher, unpublished PhD thesis, University of East Anglia.

Barnes, J. (1989) *The History of the World in Ten and a Half Chapters*, London: Picador.

Blyth, J.E. (1982) *History in Primary Schools*, London: McGraw-Hill.

Colwell, E. (1980) *Storytelling*, London: Bodley Head.

Cooper, H. (1995) *History in the Early Years*, London: Routledge.

Department of Education and Science (DES) (1967) *The Plowden Report*, London: HMSO.

Department of Education and Science (DES) (1975) *A Language for Life*, London: HMSO.

Egan, K. (1978) 'Teaching the Varieties of History', *Teaching History*, 21: 21.

Egan, K. (1979) *Educational Development*, New York: Oxford University Press.

Egan, K. (1983) 'Childrens' Path to Reality from Fantasy: Contrary Thoughts about Curriculum Foundations', *Journal of Curriculum Studies*, 15, 5: 357–71.

Egan, K. (1988) *Teaching as Story Telling: An Alternative Approach to Teaching and the Curriculum*, London and New York: Routledge.

Egan, K. (1990) *Romantic Understanding: The Development of Rationality and Imagination, Ages 8 to 15*, London and New York: Routledge.

Farmer, A. (1990) 'Story-telling in History', *Teaching History*, 58: 17–23.

Howe, A. and Johns, J. (1992) *Common Bonds: Storytelling in the Classroom*, London: Hodder and Stoughton.

Husbands, C. (1996) *What is History Teaching?*, Buckingham: Open University Press.

Lee, P. (1991) 'Historical Knowledge and the National Curriculum', in R. Aldrich (ed.), *History in the National Curriculum*, London: Kogan Page.

Lewis, K. (1994) *The Last Train*, London: Walker.

Sylvester, D. (1994) 'Change and Continuity in History Teaching, 1900–1993', in H. Bourdillon (ed.), *Teaching History*, London: Routledge.

Taylor, A.J.P. (1983) 'Fiction in History', in J. Fines (ed.), *Teaching History*, Edinburgh: Macmillan, 113–15.

Wilson, J.B. (1979) *The Story Experience*, New Jersey and London: Scarecrow Press.

4

VOICES OF THE PAST

Oral history and English in the primary curriculum

Allan Redfern

Speaking and listening with a clear sense of purpose lies at the very heart of active involvement in oral history. Talking to older people about their lived experience and recording their memories provides vivid and unique information which deepens knowledge and understanding of the past and also closely involves participants in the process of historical enquiry. This combination of knowledge, skills and understanding is central to the history National Curriculum, just as speaking and listening is a major element in the programmes of study for English. Oral history provides an important context and stimulus for reading and writing but it is on the very special relationship with speaking and listening and the promotion of quality learning here and in history that this chapter concentrates.

School children of all ages can be involved in oral history enquiry and this chapter draws on and analyses the practical experiences of teachers and pupils during history-led topics across the primary age range. Whether with year 1 or year 4, the activities examined involved pupils in the process of direct oral history enquiry relating to the lives of local people. Through examining activities with both younger and older pupils it is possible to consider progression and other age and ability issues related to planning and implementation in history and English. There is a range of valuable oral sources other than 'in the flesh' dialogues, important links with reading and writing and a range of further cross-curricular opportunities which cannot be adequately addressed here. These and more detailed practical issues are considered elsewhere (see in particular Oral History Society 1992; Perks 1992; Perks and Thompson 1997; and Redfern 1996 and 1998). Before looking more closely the value of oral history in speaking and listening and history we need to define what this activity usually involves and begin to indicate the opportunities it offers to both younger and older primary school pupils.

The nature of oral history activity

Each phase of enquiry should involve the active participation of pupils and engage them in purposeful speaking and listening. It is suggested that the fullest benefits might be gained through the following sequence of activities.

Discussing the value of oral history

Children work with greater enthusiasm if they understand the point of what they are doing, and this needs to be done at the level which best suits the particular pupils. Even with the very youngest pupils it is possible to draw on their own memories, perhaps from the previous day or 'your oldest memory', in order to show how special the information contained in memories can be. This could then be extended to specific themes which might later involve adults. It is always very useful to place memories alongside other types of evidence such as artefacts and photographs as this is an excellent way of demonstrating the unique insights that oral testimony sometimes provides. During this stage a lot of speaking and listening will have taken place and historical ideas relating to time, enquiry and interpretation will have been considered.

Learning to use the tape recorder/video camera

If testimony is to be used to its full potential it is important that interviews are recorded on audiotape or video. Pupils enjoy and gain valuable skills from the use of this technology and it is important that they are encouraged to share responsibilities for using it. At this stage, before the 'real' interviews take place they can exercise speaking and listening skills and the use of equipment by conducting group or paired interviews with each other. Children like to hear their own voices and these sessions provide an opportunity to discuss their speaking.

Identifying appropriate respondents

Talking about who might be interviewed as part of a given project can be done at various levels of sophistication and might involve a range of skills and concepts. With the youngest pupils it might simply be talking about age-related issues, for example, deciding how old people would need to be to remember particular things from the past. Older pupils would draw on a deeper range of knowledge and understanding when discussing, for instance, the range of types of people they would like to interview about experiences during Coronation Day, 1953.

Preparing questions

An ability to formulate questions is a fundamental skill which is common to both English and history and, as with identifying potential respondents, requires some background knowledge of the subject being investigated. With the youngest pupils this activity is very much a teacher–pupil discussion about the dialogue which might take place when the visitors come into school. Young pupils are quite uninhibited about asking questions but the extent to which their questions will increase their historical knowledge and understanding will depend a lot on how the teacher prepares them and how the 'interview' is managed. The teacher can help by drawing up some key questions suggested by infant pupils whereas juniors are quite capable of devising their own questions in liaison with their teacher. Such questions provide a basic framework and pupils should be encouraged to engage in a dialogue which emphasises listening and responding with additional questions.

Conducting interviews

Interviews are enjoyable and central activities to oral history, and there is a variety of ways in which they can be done. The key skills are speaking and listening within an historical context but a broad range of other skills are also involved. By interviewing each other and adults in the school, important foundations can be laid before the visit of respondents. The case studies outlined later in this chapter illustrate a variety of ways in which interviews can be conducted and an idea of what pupils of all ages can achieve.

Analysing, summarising, editing and transcribing

Once the interview is completed it is important that effective use is made of the testimony whilst it is still 'fresh in the mind' and that it does not remain locked away in a cassette. The interview can first be discussed in general terms and then listened to more closely. Again, the role and approach of the teacher is important as they can orchestrate pupil involvement according to their needs and abilities. Editing and transcribing selected testimony is also important and demands close listening, discussion and decision making (and accurate writing). After initial support older pupils are capable of doing this with increasing autonomy and are also able to index and store material. Younger pupils can be involved in selecting material and putting it into written form but will obviously need more help from adults.

Using oral testimony

Organising and communicating ideas and information are key activities in English and the final phase in the process of oral history. A particular attraction of oral history is that, once collected, the evidence can be used in exciting ways, many of which involve further use of technology and spoken forms of communication. For example, by using two tape recorders or a twin deck machine pupils can combine a variety of material (including contemporary music and old sound archive) with their own spoken commentary to produce their topic radio programme. There are also opportunities to incorporate people's memories into drama presentations, preparation for which would also involve reading and writing.

This outline of what oral history entails points to a close relationship between this approach to history and speaking and listening. However, a closer analysis is needed if teachers are to be persuaded to invest the necessary time and effort in this approach to learning. It should be stressed that the focus on speaking and listening and evidence gained through direct dialogue with older people is only part of the case for oral history across and beyond the statutory curriculum (Redfern 1996). We shall begin by summarising the contribution to history, starting with the Key Elements and then moving on to other aspects of the programme of study at each Key Stage.

The History Key Elements

Active involvement in oral history can contribute to the teaching of all five history Key Elements at levels across and beyond Key Stages 1 and 2. Brief reference to each of the them will serve to illustrate this.

Chronology

Contact with real people and aspects of their life history personalises what could otherwise be difficult abstractions and can richly illustrate change and time and the language used to describe it. Stories contained within an interview could provide an interesting foundation for a sequencing activity. Talking about the past involves pupils and adults using the vocabulary of time, and progression in the language used will reflect the timespan a particular topic entails.

Range and depth of historical knowledge and understanding

More than any other source, oral evidence provides a range and depth of knowledge about the experiences of ordinary people – men, women children and minority groups. A tremendous advantage of the dialogue aspect of this approach is that children can ask directly about reasons for and consequences of individual actions and can increasingly gain a broader understanding of cause and effect. Oral testimony provides vivid contrasts and similarities between life today and at different points in the past. Depending on the nature of the investigation, oral testimony may simply provide contrast between 'now' and 'then' or may provide details of changes across the time periods during which a respondent has lived.

Interpretations of history

Oral accounts are one way in which the past is represented and they exemplify how 'interpretations' can differ. Teachers can also show how memories are also used in other forms of interpretation, including written accounts and drama and at some museums and historical sites. With older pupils analysis of reasons for differing oral accounts and how and why they sometimes contrast with other versions provides a tangible way into more difficult facets of historical interpretation.

Historical enquiry

Oral history promotes active involvement in enquiry and is accessible to the very youngest pupils. Asking questions is fundamental to all forms of historical enquiry and is central to oral history. Other historical sources often have greater meaning or value when used in conjuction with people's memories.

Organisation and communication

There is an exciting range of literary and oral forms in which pupils can make use of people's memories. The various forms of oral communication could present special opportunities for less literate pupils.

Oral history and the programmes of study for history

Oral history can contribute to study units at each key stage, both as a source of knowledge and understanding and as a means of developing historical skills. There is a considerable range of oral evidence besides that collected by pupils (including audiovisual archives, popular music and oral material in printed form) which could help take pupils back beyond living memory and involve them in extensive speaking and listening activity. In this chapter we consider material created by our pupils but whatever the key stage, the importance and value of interrelating oral with other historical sources should always be borne in mind.

Key Stage 1

The single unit places considerable emphasis on the more recent past with a focus on: aspects of everyday life; work, leisure and culture of men, women and children; the lives of different kinds of famous men and women; and past events of different types. Each of these areas of study can be greatly enhanced through the use of oral testimony and many aspects of the past, rarely represented in published learning resources, can be better understood through the testimony of real people. When studying the cultural diversity of past societies, the experiences of minorities and ordinary men, women and children, the testimony of those people provides the major means through which their history can be explored. Interviewing can go back beyond living memory. Older people also transmit oral tradition about life before they were born and interviews with adults 'in role' would allow pupils to communicate with figures from the past. Many teachers use a 'history backwards' approach which might begin by looking at the personal history of the youngest children and draw on pupils' and parents' memories of their first five or six years.

Key Stage 2

Although other forms of oral evidence can contribute to the full range of Key Stage 2 units, the potential for direct oral history enquiry lies in the local history unit and *Britain since 1930*. Every school has potential access to local people whose lives span the *Britain since 1930* study unit and could choose to use their memories to give oral history a central role in pupils' investigations. Similarly, oral evidence could play a major part in local history if it were decided to centre investigations on themes or events within living memory. A range of factors, including the extent to which English and history were 'paired', would determine the scale of oral history activity within a topic. If such work were also seen as making a major contribution to core curriculum work in English then the effort involved would seem better justified and issues relating to the distribution of curriculum time would gain new perspectives.

The rest of this chapter argues that high-quality teaching and learning in English and history can take place simultaneously during oral history activities. Learning objectives for both history and English can be addressed but it is also important to recognise that historical enquiry is enjoyable and provides a stimulating context and real sense of purpose for speaking and listening. Examples from infant and junior classrooms exemplify these latter points.

Oral history and speaking and listening

The general requirements for speaking and listening also mirror the key facets of oral history enquiry, that pupils should be taught to:

- formulate, clarify and express their ideas; adapt their speech to a widening range of circumstances and demands;
- listen, understand and respond appropriately to others.

(DfE 1995: 2)

The contribution that oral history can make in developing effective speaking and listening and an understanding and use of the vocabulary and grammar of standard English is explored in Figures 4.1 and 4.2. As with history, the requirements for English at each key stage focus on common skills, knowledge and areas of understanding and the differences largely relate to progression. The main purpose in providing separate figures for each key stage is to demonstrate this and to aid analysis of the key stage linked case studies which follow.

These infant and junior projects, mainly from Rode Heath Primary School, Cheshire, demonstrate pupil involvement in oral history enquiry and ways in which speaking and listening were being promoted. All the projects developed knowledge of local history and drew heavily on the experiences of people in the community. The level at which historical enquiry and speaking and listening developed varied according to age and ability but there is evidence that learning in both history and speaking and listening was enhanced with all classes. These case studies look at what teacher and pupils did at each stage of their enquiries (as defined above) and what they achieved.

Case study 1: 'Old and new' topic (year 1 class)

Discussing the value of oral history

The creation of an 'old and new' museum in the classroom provided a valuable stimulus to talking about the past. Items brought in by adults and children were discussed and it was made clear to the children that they and the teacher had valuable memories associated with some of the things, but they came to understand that we needed older people to join us for really good discussion about things such as flat irons, oil lamps and old photographs (this also involved some time/chronology-related discussion aided by the use of simple timelines and the chronological layout of items on display).

Learning to use the tape recorder

We did not use a camcorder, but children became very familiar with the tape recorder as all class and group discussions were recorded. At an early stage each child spoke into the microphone, operated record/pause controls and played back the recording of their voice.

Selected statements from the English Programme of Study	The contribution of oral history
Pupils should be: given opportunities to talk for a range of purposes . . . exploring, developing and clarifying ideas . . . describing events, observations and experiences . . . giving reasons for opinions	Historical enquiry through **talking to older people** provides an exciting and meaningful **stimulus** for speaking and listening. These are real and enjoyable occasions when children can **explore** specific historical themes through **dialogue**. Recordings can be used later and observations and different ideas can be discussed
encouraged to speak with confidence, making themselves clear through organising what they say . . . taught conventions of discussion and conversation	Talking to visiting adults as part of a project will foster **oral communication skills. Organising questions** to be asked and practising the art of **interviewing** prior to the meetings will give more structure to the event and enhance the quality of the dialogue
encouraged to listen with growing attention and concentration, to respond appropriately to what they have heard and to ask and answer questions that clarify their understanding and indicate thoughtfulness about the matter under discussion	**Listening and talking are at the heart of oral history activity.** These skills are best developed through the meaningful and purposeful practical activity of the sort oral history entails. Children need to be encouraged to **listen and think** about what is being said about specific things, and oral enquiry will give them opportunities to **ask additional questions** in response to information given – this skill will develop gradually and may need prompting by interventions by the teacher (and respondent) during interviews
given opportunities to consider their own speech and how they communicate with others particularly in more formal situations or with unfamiliar adults	Recorded interviews can be subsequently used for a variety of purposes. They provide a valuable historical resource but also **opportunities for children to hear themselves speaking** (which they love to do!) during what are special occasions – this can provide a valuable source for **discussion and assessment** of individual progress
encouraged to develop confidence in their ability to adapt what they say to their listeners and to the circumstances, beginning to recognise how language differs	Interviewing often requires the **rephrasing** of a question and **adapting language** to a more formal context than usual. The adults children interview often speak in less familiar **accents** or **dialects** and this can provide a valuable introduction to the idea of standard English and the rich **diversity** of language.

Figure 4.1 Oral history and 'Speaking and Listening' at Key Stage 1

Selected statements from the English Programme of Study	The contribution of oral history
Pupils should be: given opportunities to talk for a range of purposes . . . exploring, developing and explaining . . . sharing ideas, insights and opinions . . . reporting and describing events and observations; presenting to audiences live or on tape	Junior pupils have an **enthusiasm** for oral history and a particular capacity for the activities which relate most to speaking and listening. This is one example of **activity common to both subjects** and of the good opportunities for work in foundation subjects to **interrelate** closely with key element in English. Pupils are **talking** to adults for **specific purposes** and gaining stimulating insights. The material **they create** can be used to **communicate information** and ideas in a variety of ways – not least through **oral presentation**, including **drama** and **compilations of taped material**
given opportunities to respond to a range of people . . . express themselves confidently and clearly to organise what they want to say, evaluate their own talk and reflect on how it varies	Oral history projects bring pupils into **contact with a range of people** and provide opportunities for challenging but interesting work. The learn that successful interviewing requires **organised** and **skilful questioning** and that this needs **planning** and **practice**. KS2 pupils can become quite adept at **identifying appropriate respondents and questions** to ask them and in the process of doing this are usually engaged in **lively discussion** in groups and with the teacher
taught to listen to others, questioning them to clarify what they mean, and extending and following up the ideas . . . to recall and re-present important features of an argument, talk . . . identify the gist of an account or the key points . . . to evaluate the key points	With practice and preparation junior **pupils can become very effective interviewers** and through oral history they learn that **careful listening** and asking **additional questions** in response to what they hear is an important key to success. Following an interview pupils should also be **involved in discussing** key points made and **selecting** material for further use
appreciation and use of standard English should be developed by involvement with others in activities . . . develop their understanding of the similarities and differences between written and spoken forms of standard English . . . standard and dialect forms . . . to use an increasingly varied vocabulary	School-based interviews will usually be done by **groups** of pupils and they will learn from **listening to each other** (sometimes less literary pupils shine in these situations) as well as benefiting from the **range of language** they receive from respondents. When **transcribing selected material** (which they can learn to do independently at this stage) they gain **practical experience** of **differences** in **spoken** and **written forms** of English.

Figure 4.2 Oral history and 'Speaking and Listening' at Key Stage 2

Identifying respondents

Again, this involved discussion about time and age and was aided by the museum display. Most children grasped that someone the age of gran or grandad 'matched' some of the things on display whereas they and their teacher were not old enough to really know about them.

Preparing questions

This was not done in a formal, structured way and mainly entailed talking about 'mysteries' surrounding some of the things in the museum and how certain questions to the right person might help solve them. The basic knowledge they had gained through discussion prior to visitors' arriving provided a valuable starting point for pupil–visitor dialogues later. Children's later questioning might have been improved if a general checklist had been drawn up during pre-visit discussions and individuals had been allocated specific questions. However, whilst some kind of preparation and knowledge is needed, there is a danger that too much structuring could inhibit interaction.

Conducting interviews

'Interviews' largely ran themselves and developed their own dynamics. The major 'lubricant' to dialogue stemmed from items taken from the museum display and the interplay they promoted between pupils and visitors (aided by discreet interventions from the teacher). During visits children did formulate their own questions: for example:

> What games did you play?
> Did they have like swings?
> Shops weren't the same were they?
> What petrol stations were there? (interestingly, from a five year old)

Quite a number of the children in the class were losing their milk teeth, so this probably explains the question:

> Were there dentists then?

Predominantly the contribution of these pupils who were very involved was to provide their own information on subjects being discussed rather than to pose questions. Whilst one respondent was giving her childhood memories of hot water bottles:

> They were fine as long as they didn't leak . . . but I always remember

this clinking noise as they put it in [the 'stopper'] like that – and the water used to go phisss!

One pupil intervened saying:

If you didn't have a hot water bottle you had to put a brick next to the fire, in the oven, then take it out and cool it down a little bit and put a cloth around it and put it into the bed . . . and a few weeks ago Beck [child's sister] had a cold and she had a bottle and the hot water bottle burst on her.

One visitor provided vivid and detailed information about washdays before electrical appliances; how to test and use a flat iron; information about heating water, using 'possers' and drying clothes. Pupils seemed fascinated by these details but were more articulate and detailed when talking about present-day technological aids for washday rather than asking questions about 'olden days'. Consequently teacher and visitor 'turned the tables' on the pupils by asking them to provide information about 'now' which the respondent in turn contrasted with 'then'. This stimulated a very rich dialogue which provided both depth of knowledge of the past and an under-standing of differences and the causes and effects of change. These sessions were rich in purposeful speaking and listening and were thoroughly enjoyed by all participants. One 'interview' with a grandma from South Wales held the children in spellbound dialogue for thirty-five minutes.

Analysing, summarising, editing and transcribing

This took place shortly after visits and was done largely through talking about what the children remembered best and their views on life in the past, and listening to selected extracts. Some 'special' memories were transcribed by the teacher and became part of the museum display. Pupils particularly liked the grandma from South Wales and, apart from the fund of informa-tion she gave them, there was valuable discussion about how her beautiful accent was different from that of most people who live in South Cheshire or the 'Potteries'.

Using oral testimony

Following the interviews there was a lot of discussion during which children demonstrated the extent of the knowledge, understanding and skills they had acquired. Both during and after interviews there were opportunities to address each of the Key Elements in history as well as exercise the full range of speaking and listening requirements. Not least, there was some lively debate related to 'interpretations of history'. For example, pupils had heard different perspectives on shopping in the past compared with now and had come to form, and give reasons for, their own points of view. Several children saw advantages to shopping today but one child thought past days were better because 'people walked to the shops and there were fewer cars on the roads'.

The last phase of this project involved a visit to Wigan Pier which included a specially requested 'grandma's washday' session. The children surprised museum staff with their articulate and informed responses to questions relating to objects associated with washday in the past. They could not only identify objects and talk about how they were used but were able to correct or extend what the Education Officer had to say. When she told them that spitting on a flat iron was the way to test its temperature they (unlike her and their teacher initially) showed they knew that vigorous bubbling meant it was too hot and that there were also other ways of testing temperature. The 'last straw' for the Education Officer was when one of the children made further comment on flat irons needing a cloth on the handle:

Pupil: But if you touched the handle you needed a wet cloth to thing, because if you, whatsit, put your hand over the handle, your hand would get burned!

Teacher: Very good – I forgot to mention that. You had to put a cloth round it, just like you said – that's excellent – right! You can have my job, I'll go home!

Several of the class incorporated oral testimony into pictures and short written accounts about 'when grandma was a child' but talking dominated both their investigations and the way in which they expressed understanding and knowledge. They had gained historical knowledge through purposeful speaking and listening and this in turn provided confidence, context, vocabulary and skills for their work in English.

Case study 2: Local history projects with junior pupils

The work done by these mainly year 4 pupils also involved them in each phase of oral history enquiry, but analysis of their work illustrates the considerable progression we can expect in both historical enquiry and speaking and listening skills (also indicated in Figure 4.2).

Discussing the value of oral history

In common with other Key Stage 2 local history projects, the year 4 children who studied the site of the former salt works in their village (which in 1982 became a small country park known as Rode Heath Rise) began by looking at the present and drawing on their own direct historical experience. The first lesson entailed talking about the area and what a visitor guide might include but also showed that their knowledge of change was limited. Initially, most of them assumed that the area had always been as it is now until one pupil stated: 'My grandad says there was a salt works down there once.' This provided a starting point for talking about the value of people's memories and the first of several discussions about historical clues which might be used by a 'time detective'. The teacher shared some memories of first coming to the village when the area was a disused refuse tip containing some of the remains of the salt works. The class then visited the site and with the aid of old maps, plans and some 'second-hand' oral evidence from the teacher discovered where buildings had been located. They were also introduced to a few archaeological remains. This initial enquiry provided a modest knowledge base (for example, that there had been several houses, a pub, a pumping engine and lime kilns, as well as a large salt works), stimulated a lot of curiosity and led them to realise that memories could make a valuable contribution to their research. From the outset pupils were encouraged to set the agenda for the enquiry, to discuss what they wanted to find out and how they might get answers. They wanted to know about the people living and working in the area – one pupil declared: 'Some of them could have been my relatives!' This did prove to be true for several pupils. Work on other sources such as maps, plans, photographs of buildings and salt industry artefacts had provided little information about people, and information gained from census data had been restricted to the period between 1851 and 1881. Through direct experience of other sources, classroom discussion and their later interviews, pupils progressively recognised the value of oral sources.

Learning to use the tape recorder

Most pupils were familiar with tape playback machines and were confident and enthusiastic about operating the tape recorder. Groups did practise interviews with the teacher, listened to themselves speaking and discussed ways of achieving good quality recordings.

Identifying appropriate respondents

Four groups were formed to discuss and jot down their ideas which they all pooled later on. This led to lively discussion in which they had to give reasons for their choice and respond to other ideas. They drew on their existing knowledge and learning experiences. They knew that salt making had ended around 1928, that some cottages and part of the old works collapsed into a deep brine pit in the mid-1930s and that the site had been a rubbish tip until about 1970. They decided that information about the relatively recent past could be provided by adults familiar to them, including parents, teachers and the countryside ranger, and were able to calculate how old someone would have to be to remember the salt works operating or 'the great collapse'. They also selected respondents in relation to the sorts of historical questions they wished to ask about such things as work, living conditions and recreations. They sought male and female respondents who had been employed at the salt works and the children of workers. They also felt that it would be useful to talk to someone who had lived down the valley. Eight people were eventually interviewed, half of them through pupil initiatives. The only type of respondent we failed to find was someone who had actually been employed at the salt works although a salt worker's daughter gave vivid descriptions of her father's work and his terrible injuries whilst employed there.

Preparing questions

As with identifying respondents, there was considerable emphasis on promoting discussion and pupil autonomy in decision making. Pupils proved well able to provide a fund of ideas and had decided that a set of questions was needed for when the visitors came. They recognised that 'not so old' adults or those who had lived in the village for less than twenty years might have valuable things to say about the changes on Rode Heath Rise since the end of tipping but that they would have no memories of the area at the time of the salt works. To overcome this difficulty they decided to split questions into two sections. Each of four groups organised, presented and discussed their ideas with the teacher and the other groups, and the resulting questionnaire was very much the product of their discussions (see displayed text p. 66). With other junior classes the creation of a questionnaire for a survey of life in their present-day community was a useful preliminary to creating historical questions and gaining experience of asking for information.

Conducting interviews

Each interview team conducted two interviews and the whole class were involved in a 'walkabout interview' with a man who talked with them down at the site they were studying (he had lived there with his brother and grandmother in the 1920s). During practices beforehand the teacher had been eager for them to avoid a narrow use of the questionnaire and to discuss a range of issues relating to successful interviewing/speaking and listening. It had been stressed that the 'formal' questions, which they took turns to ask, were only there to provide a basic framework and that sometimes it might be necessary to rephrase questions if there was limited response. It was also pointed out that careful listening was very important because some answers opened up new lines of enquiry. There had also been discussion relating to the social skills and sensitivities required during and after the visit of older people.

During the interviews pupils' skills and confidence grew, they established

Rode Heath C.P. School

SALT HISTORY PROJECT: INTERVIEW QUESTIONS

Part One: The recent history of Rode Heath Rise
(This section is mainly for people with less than twenty years' knowledge of the Rode Heath area.)

1   When did you first see the area where the salt works had been?
2   What was the area called then?
3   How and when did the area become known as Rode Heath Rise?
4   Were there any visible remains of the salt works when you saw the area?
5   What can you remember of the general view down the valley when you first saw it – was the shape of the valley different?
6   Do you remember anything about the rubbish tip area?
7   Do you remember the lime kilns?

Part Two: The salt works area before 1970

1   How far back do your memories of the salt works go?
2   Can you describe what the salt works looked like when you were young?
3   Do you have any memories of the salt works working?
4   Do you remember anything about the people who lived down the valley?
5   What sort of work did the men and women at the salt works do?
6   Where did the salt workers live?
7   Do you know anything about their pay, working conditions and where they shopped and got their entertainment (men and women)?
8   Do you remember anything about particular salt workers?
9   Do you remember the collapse of the salt works?
10 Can you recall anything about transport associated with the salt industry?

THANK YOU

a good rapport with their visitors and they gained very good-quality testimony. Some pupils needed prompting to ask supplementary questions but, overall, these pupils really were interviewing, and with a clearly defined sense of purpose. Many were quite capable of pursuing a theme further than the respondent's initial answer by rephrasing questions. One of the girls who was interviewing an elderly man with direct knowledge of the salt works had a particular interest in women's wages in the 1920s and refused to be put off with a 'simplistic' answer. First she asked an additional question about wages:

Pupil: Were wages a lot lower for women?
Respondent: Oh a lot lower my love, women were very poorly paid – in those days right at the bottom of the scale.

The pupil was interrupted at this point by another child too eager to ask the next question, but at the first opportunity she sought a fuller explanation:

Pupil: Do you know why it was so – that men got paid more than women. Do you know why men got paid more than women?

The respondent was somewhat taken aback by the pupil's obvious determination to pursue the issue and seemed to view the child as a future fighter for people's rights. He began his response by saying to her:

Just listen to what I'm telling you now because you will grow up yourself like that some day.

and treated the group to a splendid account of the suffragettes and other struggles for equality during the opening decades of the century. This was a direct result of the questioning skills and determination of an eight-year-old girl.

Analysing, summarising, editing and transcribing

These activities require careful listening and benefit from group and whole-class discussion, but junior pupils can work increasingly independently in these areas, hearing and discussing their own 'performance'. The groups reported back and played selected extracts for closer discussion with the teacher and the rest of the class. They transcribed fairly short selected extracts and found it challenging to convert spoken language into written form. Their efforts were modest but certainly began to extend their listening skills for new purposes.

Using oral testimony

Some extracts were used as part of a piece of individual written work in the form of an account of a typical day for a salt worker. For example, several pupils made references to the dehydrating conditions in the works and the fondness and capacity of certain workers (usually themselves 'in role') for large quantities of Guinness (which they had heard about from one particularly informative interviewee). They also produced an assembly presentation which included a 'scene' recreating life at the works making use of selected memories. At another school a class recruited the help of local radio stations when compiling an audio presentation of extracts, music and commentary relating to their village during the Second World War. Several schools published local histories based almost entirely on collected oral testimony.

Conclusion

Through the context of both infant and junior projects this chapter has analysed and demonstrated the close links between oral history activity and the development of speaking and listening. These links have been further emphasised by reference to the relationship between the skills of oral history and specific statutory requirements for English in the National Curriculum. What did shine out in these projects was the tremendous enthusiasm which pupils at all levels of ability showed for their work. Pupils worked with a sense of purpose in a historical context which stimulated their interest and imagination. They had reasons for engaging in dialogue which in turn enhanced knowledge and confidence in subsequent activities. Put simply, they came to understand much better the value of asking questions and the benefits of listening. Their interviews were important occasions which gave them a sense of achievement, the feeling that they had created something unique and special and, perhaps most importantly, a feeling of collective ownership of what they had done. When pupils respond in these ways teachers will know that they are on to a good thing.

References

Department for Education (DfE) (1995) *English in the National Curriculum*, London: HMSO.

Oral History Society (1992) Special 'National Curriculum' edition, *Oral History: Journal of the Oral History Society*, 20, 1.

Perks, R. (1992) *Oral History: Talking About the Past*, London: Historical Association.

Perks, R. and Thompson, A. (1997) *The Oral History Reader*, London: Routledge.

Redfern, A.R. (1996) *Talking in Class: Oral History and the National Curriculum*, Colchester: Oral History Society.

Redfern, A.R. (1998) 'Living with the National Curriculum', *Oral History: Journal of the Oral History Society*, 26, 1.

5

CHILDREN WORKING WITH PICTURES

Penelope Harnett

The place of pictures in learning history

The purpose of this chapter is to describe some of the ways in which pictures can enhance children's learning in history. It begins with an historical perspective describing how pictures have been used for teaching history in the past. The chapter discusses the importance of visual literacy for learning about history and explores how children approach historical pictures and develop their historical understanding. Language plays a central role in helping children to organise their historical experiences and to communicate their understanding to others. Throughout the chapter examples of children's language will be included to illustrate aspects of historical learning. The chapter concludes by discussing ways of working in the classroom and the role of the teacher in structuring children's learning and resourcing historical activities.

Pictures and history: an historical perspective

The wealth of pictures, both photographs and artists' illustrations now available for teaching history, is striking and contrasts with the limited range and variety available earlier in the century. Authenticity and historical accuracy have not always featured strongly in many artists' illustrations. Indeed, one author of a history teaching textbook lamented: 'If you draw Alexander, do at least make him look like a Greek and not a Roman' (Firth 1929). There were few photographs and reprographic techniques limited the value of black and white photographs as sources of information since they often had fuzzy outlines and were small and dark. Other visual sources included black line drawings; some were very sketchy and indistinct whereas others, notably by the Quennells (1931), were careful copies of primary sources.

In the primary years, history was often taught through stories, using large posters linked to the story which aimed to provide the children with a sense of the period (often an inaccurate one), and to fire their imaginations. In the decades following the Second World War, children's history books were enlivened with more coloured illustrations. Perhaps the best-known were Unstead's series of history books which included black and white line drawings and some coloured illustrations. Artists' illustrations continued to dominate primary history books published in the 1960s and 1970s.

Currently, although artists' illustrations remain popular, photographs of historical objects, buildings and paintings are also more readily available. The inclusion of photographs is due partly to improvements in reprographic techniques, but also to the fact that since the introduction of the history National Curriculum there has been a greater emphasis on the value of pictures as sources of historical information which can be used as evidence of ways of life in the past. Learning through pictures is recognised as an important way of developing children's historical skills as well as their historical understanding and knowledge. Pictures can provide children with immediate overall impressions of life in the past, as well as opportunities for more in-depth study and detailed historical research.

The importance of visual literacy

Representing ideas

Pictures offer powerful ways of representing knowledge and understanding. Complex and abstract ideas which have a direct impact on the viewer can be portrayed through visual media. In the past, for example, medieval paintings revealed the mysteries of heaven and hell to a non-literate population. The grotesque and fearsome monsters from hell depicted in the paintings were vivid reminders to people of their own mortality and the power of evil. As such, these images were effective representations of contemporary understanding of the world.

In our current more literate society, pictures continue to convey powerful messages – a fact often exploited by advertisers. Particular images are used to sell products and to influence people's ideas. The amounts of money poured into advertising companies reveal people's beliefs in the effectiveness of the visual image.

Pictorial representation is one of the three characteristic ways of representing and learning about the world described by Bruner (1966). The iconic mode of learning (seeing the world visually through pictures, maps, plans and so on) is included alongside the enactive (understanding by doing and experience) and the symbolic (representing ideas, concepts and knowledge through language). These three modes all provide important ways of learning and Bruner suggests that children should be taught to function effectively across these different modes.

The current history National Curriculum provides opportunities for children to experience all three modes of learning: pictures and maps are included as important sources of evidence within Key Element 4, and children's awareness of the passage of time and chronology is developed through visual representations of time lines, family trees and so on (iconic mode). Children learn within the symbolic mode as they work with documents and different historical texts. Their active involvement is encouraged as they interpret different sources in an attempt to reconstruct the past (enactive mode).

Research and visual literacy

Our knowledge of the value of pictures in developing children's understanding in primary history owes much to the work of John West. West developed activities with children to encourage them to work as real historians, using pictures as sources of information. He concluded that children were capable of acquiring the concept of evidence and of recognising authenticity. Using pictures for sequencing activities, West (1986) noted children's abilities to recognise cause and effect and to empathise with people from the past. Particularly significant were children's powers of observation and deduction.

Research by Blyth (1988) also indicated how pictures could contribute towards children's historical understanding. Children were asked to explain what was happening in the pictures which Blyth asked them to look at. Talking through the pictures, Blyth noted that nine-year-old children were able to engage with abstract historical concepts such as change, power, sequence and evidence.

Children's abilities to recognise significant features and to make generalisations about past ways of life from historical pictures progresses as they gain more experience from picture reading. In her research with groups of children aged five, seven, nine and eleven, Harnett (1993) noted that the younger children tended to observe pictures in minute detail, recounting everything which they could see in them. Older children, however were more able to view a picture in its entirety and to draw conclusions about the past from their observations. This was further supported by later research which indicated that children progressed from focusing questions on particular details to general impressions when they used pictures as sources of evidence (Harnett 1996).

A number of studies have demonstrated the value of using pictures for developing children's sequencing skills and their abilities to describe the passage of time. West introduced his washing line with pegs into the classroom, and this enabled children to organise their sequence of pictures and to move them around as they reviewed their decisions. Harnett (1993) investigated some of the difficulties which children experience as they sequence pictures and emphasised the importance of developing children's vocabulary of time to enable them to explain their sequence and to express their understanding in terms which can be universally understood. (This is addressed further in Chapter 7.)

Lynn (1993) noted that young children aged six to seven years do not identify specific historical clues when they sequence pictures, but rather rely on the brightness of the picture. Dull-toned and black and white pictures invariably were placed further back in time than coloured pictures. This led to some startling ways of organising pictures, including placing a coloured photograph of the Ancient Egyptians as being more recent than a sepia-toned photograph of family life in the 1930s. As children grew older, however, Lynn suggested that they were less likely to create such stereotypes based on colour and black and white images.

Language and learning

Learning: moving forward in our understanding

We learn about the past from many experiences both inside and outside school. It is a continuous process as we seek to make sense of our experiences and construct our own understanding of the world. Piaget made the useful distinction between new ideas which can be assimilated within existing conceptual frameworks and other new ideas which require us to accommodate them by changing our existing understanding. Accommodation occurs as we modify our current understanding to take into account fresh ideas and experiences.

Whereas Piaget has tended to emphasise learning as a process whereby individuals construct their own unique interpretation of the world (see Ginsburg and Opper 1969), the work of other psychologists such as Vygotsky (1978) and Bruner (1966) have emphasised the social nature of learning. We construct our own views of the world but this is in the context of our culture and in response to existing members of our community. We learn more from each other than we could achieve on our own. Vygotsky (1978: 86) introduces the notion of the zone of proximal development (ZPD), which he describes as 'the distance between the actual level [of the child] as determined through problem-solving and the level of potential development as determined through problem-solving under adult guidance or in collaboration with more capable peers'. Intervention and support from more knowledgeable others enables us to move forward in our understanding across the ZPD.

Learning and language: the importance of talk

As we reshape our knowledge and understanding we try out new ideas and new ways of thinking. Language can play a central role in this process. It can be used as an organising tool which enables us to explore and to sort out our ideas and experiences – a sort of 'personal thinking tool'. Language also enables us to communicate our ideas to others, to arrive at shared under-standings – 'a shared communication tool'. Moreover, as we communicate with others, either our peers or other adults, we are exposed to alternative viewpoints, providing different interpretations which can extend our ideas and provide fresh information and knowledge.

In the examples from classrooms which follow, the role of talk in enhancing children's learning in history is explored, together with the role of the teacher in planning and organising activities which promote talk. The activities which are described have strong links with the English National Curriculum Programmes of Study. In particular, they meet the general requirements for developing effective speaking and listening (DfE 1995: 2) through encouraging children to:

- formulate, clarify and express their ideas;
- adapt their speech to a widening range of circumstances and demands;
- listen, understand and respond appropriately to others.

Reading pictures: developing understanding

Personal frameworks

Reception and year 1 children looked at a variety of pictures of Queen Elizabeth II and the royal family to extend their knowledge about the monarchy and to develop their understanding of important people. A group of reception children looked at pictures of the present Queen involved in ceremonial duties and were then asked about the sort of work which she does. They were encouraged to describe what they saw in the different pictures. The teacher taped the children's responses to the discussion:

A: She cleans the house.
Teacher: What else does she do?
A: Lay the table.
Teacher: Lays the table.
S: Shuts the windows when they're open.
Teacher: Yes. It would get very draughty if she didn't shut the windows. Anything else?
S: Shut the curtains.
Teacher: Shuts the curtains.
M: Makes the beds.
Teacher: Have any of you seen her on television? What does she do on television?
P: I see her on the stair.
M: Someone is guarding her.

Despite the fact that the children had viewed pictures of the Queen in her carriage, opening Parliament, attending the trooping of the colour and presiding at a state banquet, the children had associated the Queen's work with household tasks – they viewed the Queen as a sort of adopted granny. These young children had interpreted the pictures within the light of their own limited experience. They had not adjusted their existing understanding to take into account fresh information and experiences.

The experience which children bring to the learning situation is very powerful in helping them to make sense of fresh information. In the example above, the teacher listened to the children's views. She valued the children's ideas by reiterating some of their comments and providing an appropriate language model, for example: lays the table; makes the beds. The teacher also provided additional comments such as 'It would get very draughty if she didn't shut the windows', in response to some of the children's ideas. She encouraged the children to think of other possibilities: 'Anything else?', and to draw on their other experiences, by reminding them that they might have seen the Queen on television. This intervention shifted the content of children's responses away from household tasks to other possibilities. P's and M's final utterances illustrate how their thinking might have been beginning to develop along other lines.

Extending children's experiences

The example above reveals how a more knowledgeable other (in this case the teacher) attempted to move the children further in their learning through the zone of proximal development. The role of the teacher in supporting children's learning is illustrated further in the following discussion. Children were talking about a picture of the Queen reviewing the trooping of the colour. It was evident that the Queen was sitting on an animal but the teacher was surprised when P thought it was a donkey:

Teacher: Do you think it's a donkey or a horse?
P: Think it's a donkey.
S: Donkey.
Teacher: Why do you say donkey?
P: . . . because it's grey.
Teacher: Do you think a donkey's very big?
All: No.
Teacher: Do you think a Queen would fit on a donkey?
All: No . . . yes.
Teacher: When you see donkeys, who generally rides donkeys? Who rides donkeys?
P: Little people.
Teacher: Little people or children on the sands.

P: Yes, because I went on one.
Teacher: Did you? Do you think it would have been big enough for a grown-up?
P: Yes.
M: Yes. People in Africa ride on them.
Teacher: Yes, they do.
S: My mum's been on a donkey.

Despite many prompts from the teacher, the children remained convinced that the Queen was sitting on a donkey. Moreover, the children supported each other in this belief. Both M and S agreed with P's assertion that grown-ups ride on donkeys, citing examples from their personal knowledge of Africa and their mum. The teacher encouraged the children to justify their comments and through her questioning provided suggestions to help children to adjust their views and consider alternative animals. She identified with children's existing understanding and tried to move them on from there.

Faced with fresh experiences, these children were constantly trying to relate them to some of their more familiar understandings. This is a process which engages all learners and is a way of working which is particularly encouraged within the history National Curriculum. Key Element 2 describes how children should compare and contrast past events and ways of life with more familiar experiences. Identifying similarities and differences introduces children to ideas that the past is different from the present. In this respect, pictures can provide children with ideal opportunities to make comparisons. They are readily accessible and most children can make some response to visual materials.

Children supporting each other

Older children have more experience and, as they work through the study units at Key Stage 2, greater historical knowledge to draw on as they seek to make sense of the world. The children in the following example had already spent some time studying the Tudor period before they were asked to work with Tudor portraits. Pairs of year 5 (9–10 year-old) children were given different portraits of Queen Elizabeth I to discuss. They were then asked to report their findings to a larger group and the teacher made notes on how the children worked together.

G and P focused their initial discussion on the organisation of their work; they agreed to take some notes to remind them of points they wanted to raise when reporting back:

G: I know what, I'll count. You'd better write, 'cos you're a better writer than me, aren't you?
P: Yes.

Figure 5.1 Portrait of Queen Elizabeth I by Marcus Gheeraerts
Source: By courtesy of the National Portrait Gallery, London

G: 'Cos otherwise I'll just end up scribbling.

P: I know, I'll do the picture this side and anything you notice on that side you put down.

This sharing of tasks continued throughout the activity, and they consulted each other on what they were going to do. G asked if he should check what colour eyes Elizabeth had, and P organised the counting of the various jewels. Once he had ascertained that there were 138 diamonds on his side of the picture he suggested multiplying the number by two to find the total. But the potential difficulties in this procedure were raised when his partner G asked: 'Did you count the ones which were a half like this one here?' The children discussed Queen Elizabeth's dress, paying great attention to its detail. They looked at her fan and facial characteristics and noted the background of the portrait.

As they worked together, they sorted out their ideas and looked to each other for confirmation and support:

G: . . . she had a heart-shaped frill around the back, 'cos look, that's a heart-shaped frill isn't it?

P: No, it's not heart-shaped, it just goes round like a semicircle.

G: Yes. It's not heart-shaped.

P: She had a round frill on her back.

The children corrected each other and returned to the picture to verify some of their observations. There was some dispute about the colour of Elizabeth's gloves:

P: Gold and white gloves.

G: Gold and white – what are you on about?

P: Golden and brown.

G: Gold and brown.

G finally concluded that they were pale brown and dark brown.

Through talk the children were able to organise their work and clarify some of their observations. They used exploratory talk to try out some of their ideas and to focus on some of the points which interested them – including the size of Queen Elizabeth's nose! Such exploratory talk was less in evidence, however, when the children reported back to each other within a larger group. In this instance there was less tentativeness in some of their observations, less questioning and fewer pauses in their dialogue.

Explaining observations to others

Explaining observations to others unfamiliar with the picture provides an incentive for children to observe closely and also to consider the language which they use to make their descriptions clear. Children engaged in the activity described below had been working on the Romans for a term and the activity was designed to extend their awareness of Roman ways of life. Pairs of year 3 children (7–8 year-olds) were given half a picture of a Roman kitchen to describe to the pair with the other half. The picture was a museum reconstruction (Figure 5.2). Along one side was a row of shelves with an assortment of pots of various sizes. A table was in the centre and on it were other pots, a sieve and a pestle and mortar surrounded by vegetables and foodstuffs. There was also an amphora and a cooking grill.

Both pairs of children engaged enthusiastically with this activity and listened well to each others' accounts. To begin with, each pair organised themselves for the task ahead. One pair took it in turns to make a comment; the children in the other pair took turns to describe the different objects in the picture.

The activity encouraged the children to describe the objects in the kitchen very carefully, to think about the language which they were using and how it might be understood by the listener. Pots were described in great detail: 'Above the bowl which has the stand and the flat wooden pestle there's a

Figure 5.2 Roman kitchen: these pots have been arranged as they might have been in a Roman kitchen.
Source: St Alban's Museum Service

brown pottery bowl. It almost looks like paint really. It's a very nice normal brown and it's very shiny and you can see the light has reflected off it. It doesn't seem . . . and it has only got one cut or chip on the stand near the bottom.' Another pair explained in great detail the appearance of the sieve and how they thought it would be used.

Locational terms were important: children's comments were regularly prefaced with phrases such as 'on the right-hand side', 'very close to', and prepositions such as below, next, underneath and above. Children counted the number of pots, vegetables and other foods. Such specificity was important as the audience was unfamiliar with the picture.

Raising questions

Young children are capable of identifying a vast amount of detail from visual sources. Recognising which features might be significant, however, develops as children gain greater experience in picture reading and more historical knowledge (Harnett 1993). This point is illustrated from work with another group of 7–8 year-olds who were invited to think of questions concerning the Roman kitchen, with the teacher acting as a scribe. The children's initial questions recorded their first impressions:

> Did they have fresh dead birds?
> Did they have shiny raisins?
> Did they have sausages?
> Did they have salami?
> Were most of their things made out of pottery?
> Did they have baskets?
> Is this a kitchen?

These questions are all very 'closed' and could all have been answered by a quick glance at the picture. The teacher then intervened and asked the children to consider the picture as providing information about the Roman way of life: what questions would they like to ask? The following three questions suggest that the children were beginning to consider the reliability of the source – did the kitchen represent an authentic reconstruction?

> Did they only mix with pestles?
> Did they only have pans?
> Did the kitchen normally have most of their tools made of wood?

The remaining questions also reveal that the children were using the picture more as a source of information about past ways of life. They were looking beyond immediate impressions and using the picture to speculate about life in Roman Britain:

Did it smell?
Did they have coal or a wood store?
How did they make things?
Did they make things themselves?
How did they make things like this out of stone?
Why didn't they have lights?
Why didn't the cups have handles?

The later questions reveal how the teacher's intervention encouraged the children to extend their thinking and range of questions. Figure 5.3 provides a useful structure for considering possible progression in children's thinking. The children's initial questions were on the first rung of the ladder. Teacher support, however, enabled the children to consider other questions linked to ways of thinking on some of the higher rungs.

Historical explanations

Several examples from the transcripts reveal that some children were developing an awareness of the tentative nature of historical enquiry. As she looked at the Roman kitchen, one child described a large pot 'which probably contains something smaller', and she added alternative explanations for a pattern: 'It could have been a pattern and could have been washed off,

Steps to thinking

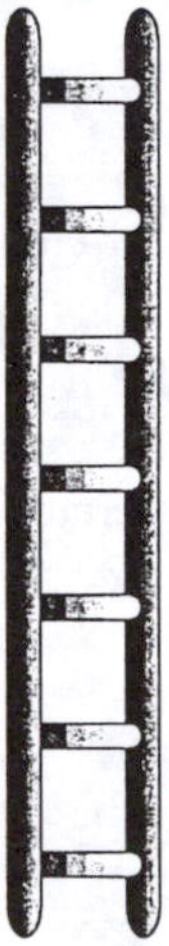

7 Apply the knowledge gained to new situations and make generalisations

6 Make judgements about and give opinions on

5 Predict and explain consequences and effects

4 Suggest causes, look for reasons

3 Compare, seek similarities and differences

2 Undertake appropriate classifications

1 Identify and describe the idea

Figure 5.3 Generating historical thinking
Source: Kimber *et al.* (1995: 177)

but it could just have been one marking.' Use of such words and phrases as 'probably', 'might have', 'could have' suggest that children were beginning to recognise how 'historical knowledge' is constructed and the essentially interpretative nature of historical processes (see Chapter 2).

This point is further illustrated as the children discussed with their teacher how the kitchen had been created. They were familiar with the work of archaeologists in piecing together different pieces of information, and one child explained the kitchen's reconstruction: 'Because if they found the kitchen they might have found different things in different places.' Another child added: 'And maybe they thought well this pot looks slightly like this (*indicating with hand gestures*). If they found something that wasn't actually with it, then they might have guessed, well, if all these pots are arranged like this then this will probably go here. Unless they want it to be completely changed.'

Interpreting sources

In relating the pots with each other, these children reveal some awareness of the nature of archaeological evidence. They recognised, too, that the food would have left few remains. So how did the archaeologists know what to include in the kitchen reconstruction? One child suggested that the archaeologist might have referred to Roman shopping lists, and his friend supported this idea by adding: 'There might be shopping lists left out at the place where there was a volcano which exploded' (the children had previously watched a programme about Pompeii).

These children are beginning to cross-reference different sources of information in their reconstruction of the past, building on their different experiences and learning. A more critical analysis of the different sources was undertaken by the group of year 5 children looking at different portraits of Elizabeth I. After they had conducted their initial investigation in pairs and reported back to the rest of the group, the children began to compare and contrast their different portraits. The portraits included: the Ditchley portrait where Elizabeth is portrayed in a magnificent gown standing on the map of England, bringing light and banishing dark storm clouds away in the background; Queen Elizabeth's coronation portrait; and a portrait of the Queen being carried on a litter surrounded by her courtiers.

The teacher introduced the idea that portraits were often created to present particular messages and the children began suggesting what impression the Queen was trying to convey. The Ditchley portrait provoked comments on her power and authority. It was as if, 'I'm the Queen – do this or I'll chop your head off'. The children noted the increasing splendour of the clothes and of the number of jewels as the Queen grew older. They attributed this to Elizabeth's increasing wealth: 'That's because when she was first crowned there, that's when she was first getting taxes to order and there that's after fifty years of taxes going towards their palace and the stuff she wears.'

Written accounts of Elizabeth's appearance were presented to the children, who were invited to contrast them with the portraits and to comment on the accuracy of the accounts. G felt that an unflattering account from a German writer was the most likely to be true, "cos he's not a British and she's not his Queen'.

Used in this way, children were able to consider the significance of different features in the portraits and to develop skills in interpretation and inference. Children's knowledge and understanding of the Elizabethan period was also extended together with their awareness of more abstract concepts such as monarchy and power. The children became familiar with specific historical vocabulary, for example: orb and sceptre; farthingale; litter; and learned how to use such words in appropriate contexts.

Very young children can also be helped to consider the significance of particular features in a picture. The reception and year 1 children were all asked to think about what things they could see in the pictures of our present Queen which made her look important and to include them in the pictures which they were asked to draw. Their comments do reveal that some of the children were beginning to recognise the importance of certain details, such as jewellery, crown, earrings, dress, necklace, hat (crown, correction by another child), although one might question whether lipstick, eyebrows and mouth were particularly important. One child generalised that it was everything that looked ''spensive' (expensive). Children also included some of these features in the pictures which they drew of the queen. During the discussion the teacher was also able to develop children's understanding

Figure 5.4 'The Queen has a crown on her head': year 1 child's drawing

Figure 5.5 'She is beautiful': year 1 child's drawing

of specific vocabulary such as crown, sword, queen, prince, princess, palace, royal family.

Teacher intervention and support

In the examples from schools used in this chapter we can see how different children have been able to engage with visual materials to develop their learning in history. Through talk, children have been able to clarify their ideas and to communicate their understanding. Children have supported each other as they have worked together in their different groups. Listening to children's talk has enabled teachers to assess children's current knowledge and to use this as a base for extending their learning. This might arise as teachers encourage children to look more closely at particular features in a picture or to consider their significance. Teachers might suggest alternative ways of viewing the pictures and at other times might intervene to provide children with additional information and further sources to help their investigations.

Effective group work occurs when children are clear about the purpose of the activity and what they are trying to achieve. Teachers have a major responsibility in structuring appropriate tasks to promote historical learning. Different activities will promote different responses and different kinds of learning. For example, pictures can be used to draw comparisons between the past and present. Children's skills in interpretation can be developed though the provision of a variety of pictures and other sources to cross-reference or children could be encouraged to identify false/true statements about a particular picture. Sequencing skills can be developed as children organise pictures to recount a particular event or place a variety of objects in chrono-logical order.

Sorting activities with pictures can also be used to provide children with an overview of a particular period of history and to recognise connections between different features of life. Riley (1997) describes a medieval picture-hunting game in which groups of children are asked to establish criteria and categorise a range of pictures about medieval life. Having selected pictures for their own category, the children then examine each others' sets of pictures. The children are allowed to remove pictures from other groups, provided they leave a calling card with the name of their category to replace the picture. As the activity progresses the interconnections between different features of the period become more apparent. In this way, picture sorting becomes an effective device enabling children to identify key features of a period and also to recognise how they interrelate with each other.

Children can be encouraged to identify significant details in the picture by labelling them and providing the picture with a caption. Roberts (1997) suggests ways in which children's written work can be developed through pictorial writing frames. Different features are selected from a picture and children asked to write about them.

Table 5.1 provides some examples of activities using pictures which relate to the different history Key Elements and which at the same time promote the development of skills in language.

Table 5.1 Opportunities for developing the history Key Elements

Key Element 1	Arrange a series of pictures in a sequence to tell the story of an event. Organise pictures on a time line and discuss why they have been arranged in a particular order.
Key Element 2	Use pictures to talk about ways of life in the past. Identify similarities and differences with the present. Identify the main features of a picture by tracing over them in outline and labelling them. Identify with the people in the picture. Tell the story about what is happening in the picture. Discuss the people's feelings and what they are doing. Interview the people in the picture.
Key Element 3	On what evidence have artists based their illustration? Compare different pictures of the same scene – say how and why they are different. Discuss whether artists' illustrations provide accurate representations of life in the past. Devise a title for the picture – compare children's different titles.
Key Element 4	Use pictures as sources of information about the past – what do they tell us about past ways of life? Relate information from pictures to other sources of information. Is it a reliable source of evidence? Encourage children to become familiar with a wide range of pictorial sources, for example, paintings, portraits, illustrations, photographs, cartoons, advertisements, woodcuts, prints and so on. Discuss how the picture was made. Who made it and for whom? Why was the picture made? Why has the picture survived? Complete a picture by drawing in any missing parts.
Key Element 5	Sort and group pictures to help children organise historical information in different ways. Use pictures to provide concrete examples to help children become familiar with more abstract historical concepts. Use pictures as a stimulus to encourage children to communicate their understanding in different ways, for example, drawing, painting, modelling, collage work, photography, talking, writing, acting, or miming.

References

Antonouris, G. and Wilson, J. (1989) *Equal Opportunities in Schools: New Dimensions in Topic Work*, London: Cassell.

Blyth, J. (1988) *History 5–9*, London: Hodder and Stoughton.

Bruner, J. (1966) *Towards a Theory of Instruction*, Cambridge, Mass.: Harvard University Press.

Department of Education (DfE) (1995) *Key Stages 1 and 2 of the National Curriculum*, London: HMSO.

Firth, C. (1929) *The Learning of History in Elementary Schools*, London: Kegan Paul, Trench Trubner.

Ginsburg, H. and Opper, S. (1969) *Piaget's Theory of Intellectual Development: An Introduction*, Englewood Cliffs, N.J.: Prentice-Hall.

Harnett, P. (1993) 'Identifying Progression in Children's Understanding: the Use of Visual Materials to Assess Primary School Children's Learning in History', *Cambridge Journal of Education*, 23, 2: 137–54.

Harnett, P. (1996) 'Questions about the Past: Responses to Historical Pictures from Primary School Children', *Welsh Historian*, 25: 19–21.

Kimber, D., Clough, N., Forrest, M., Harnett, P., Menter, I. and Newman, E. (1995) *Humanities in Primary Education*, London: Fulton.

Lynn, S. (1993) 'Children Reading Pictures: History Visuals at Key Stages 1 and 2', *Education 3–13*, 21, 3: 23–30.

Norman, K. (1990) *Teaching, Talking and Learning in Key Stage 1*, York: National Curriculum Council.

Quennell, M. and Quennell, C.H.B. (1931) *Everyday Things in Archaic Greece*, London: Batsford.

Riley, M. (1997) 'Big Stories and Big Pictures: Making Outlines and Overviews Interesting', *Teaching History*, 88: 20–22.

Roberts, N. (1997) *Roman Britain, Part 1: Source Materials for use in the Primary School Classroom*, Wisbech, Cambs.: School's Library of Historical Source Material.

Vygotksy, L.S. (1978) *Mind in Society: The Development of Higher Psychological Processes*, Cambridge, Mass.: Harvard University Press.

West, J. (1986) 'The Development of Primary School Children's Sense of the Past: History And The Primary School, *Greater Manchester Primary Contact*, Special Issue no. 6.

6

HISTORY AND CHILDREN'S FICTION

Kath Cox and Pat Hughes

> Story has long been considered an appropriate method of
> teaching history to infants. A good, well-told story commands
> attention and can lead to discussion, question and answer. The
> attraction of story lies in its narrative power, through which it
> appeals to children's curiosity, emotions and imagination.
>
> (NCC 1993: 33)

The link between story and history is a long-established one. For thousands
of years communities have learnt about their past through the medium of
story. In early times these stories were passed on by storytellers as part of the
oral tradition. With the coming of literacy, the stories were written down and
became accessible to those who could read. There are many adults in Britain
today who remember learning history at school by listening to or reading the
'true' stories of famous men (few women), daring deeds, significant events
and dates. More able and avid readers at school may have ventured into the
world of historical fiction and found that these stories brought the past to
life in a different way by bringing human dilemmas, decisions and feelings
into what could often be a barren landscape of battles, treaties and laws. In
this chapter we consider the value of story, and specifically the use of fiction,
for history teaching in primary schools. The place of fiction in the changing
programmes of study for history at Key Stages 1 and 2 is reviewed briefly.
Then, using examples of children's fiction, we suggest how stories can be
used to support the development of historical knowledge and understanding
at Key Stages 1 and 2 through activities which support the acquisition of
literacy skills. Finally, we look to the future and consider how the increasing
emphasis on structured literacy teaching may impact on the place of story in
history teaching.

What does story offer history?

- Stories offer a means of introducing children to 'different worlds' beyond their own experience – to the world of the past.
- Through exploring the beliefs and actions of characters in stories children can begin to appreciate the feelings and motivation of people – ordinary people and those with power.
- Stories can act as a vehicle for historical vocabulary – introducing new words or providing children with a context for terms introduced through other activities such as work with sources.
- Stories provide a vehicle for introducing children to ideas that might be too difficult or sensitive when presented in a more formal context (Claire 1996).
- A good story can have a major impact on the affective domain, creating interest and excitement, and promoting an emotional response from children.
- Stories can provoke questions which need additional research or work with sources if they are to be answered.
- The internal chronology and narrative form of story provide children with support to order and recount the past.
- Where stories are accompanied by illustrations, further information about the time depicted can be conveyed through the pictures thus contributing to children's mental images of the past.

Story and history at Key Stage 1

The potential contribution of story, particularly for Key Stage 1 pupils, was identified in the early deliberations in preparation for the National Curriculum orders. The final report of the History Working Party suggested that teachers 'use stories . . . as a major source of knowledge about the past for young pupils' (DES 1990: 35). Seven categories of story were listed as appropriate. Reflecting a variety of cultures and periods, they were to include 'stories about the past read or told at story-time' – interpreted as referring to children's fiction. By the time that these initial guidelines had been consolidated into the final orders (DES 1991a) the earlier list had been pruned – for reasons of simplification and possibly reflecting the views of 'purists' who were and are unconvinced about the place of story. However, the status of story within the programme of study for Key Stage 1 was clearly indicated by the opening paragraph which set out the Key Elements:

> Pupils should be helped to develop an awareness of the past through stories from different periods and cultures, including:
>
> well-known myths and legends;
> stories about historical events;

eye-witness accounts of historical events;
fictional stories set in the past.

(DES 1991a: 13)

Statement of attainments for Attainment Target 1 (knowledge and under-standing of history) indicated that stories have a specific role in developing children's understanding of chronology through sequencing (level 1). In Attainment Target 2 (interpretations of history) stories would promote children's awareness that characters could be real or fictional (level 1), and that there could be different versions of what happened (level 2). However, significant changes in the terminology were noted. Stories would now help children develop an 'awareness' of, rather than acquire 'knowledge' about, the past. This shift in emphasis may be attributed to the influence of those who were (and still are) less happy about the role of story generally in history teaching. Two main areas of criticism can be found. Academic historians have been 'dismissive of mere story: an unacademic, slightly immature and unreliable mode of analysis' (Husbands 1996: 46). Those involved with teaching school history have viewed the story approach as representing methods associated with 'the great tradition of the history teacher relaying mainly British, mainly political history to essentially passive pupils' (ibid.). (For a fuller discussion see ibid., ch. 4.) These views may also go some way to explain the contrasting status afforded story in general and historical fiction in particular in the Key Stage 2 programme of study. Reviewing links between English and history, the History Working Party suggested that historical fiction can be 'helpful as a source, but it needs careful handling' (DES 1990: 181). In the Final Orders two direct references appear. In the section detailing links with Attainment Targets (ATs) stories are suggested as a way of developing 'awareness of different ways of representing past events' (AT2). 'Fictional accounts' are included in the range of historical sources from which pupils might gain information (AT3) (DES 1991a: 16). The *Non-statutory Guidance* (DES 1991b) contains scattered references. Thus we learn in the section dealing with AT2 that 'historical novelists' produce interpretations of the past (ibid.: 6). Neither the consultation report nor the Final Orders identify to a satisfactory degree the potential of fiction at Key Stage 2, ignoring the findings of those interested in this area (Little and John 1986)

The emphasis on story in Key Stage 1 history teaching was welcomed by those working with younger pupils. 'Story time' was a daily occurrence in most infant classrooms, albeit with a focus on the development of English skills. Thus it was an approach with which teachers felt comfortable. Children would be able to apply their accumulated knowledge about story structure, narrative and picture reading to books with an historical focus. The explicit advice to use children's fiction was even more welcome as it enabled existing book resources to be used. For example, the illustrations for

Peepo (Ahlberg 1981) could be used to provide information about ordinary life fifty years ago. Further support came from publications providing guidance to help teachers identify the historical potential of stories and ensure that the examples of children's fiction chosen encouraged the development of children's historical knowledge, concepts and skills (Cox and Hughes 1990; Gadsden 1991).

Educational publishers took note of the resource implications of the Final Orders and teachers' growing enthusiasm for using stories for history. In the period since 1991 there has been a steady increase in the range of suitable stories available for Key Stage 1 history. Expert authors were commissioned to write stories about real people and events that could be read by the children themselves (Benjamin 1996; Potter 1996). However, some seemed designed as additions to existing reading schemes rather than texts written with the criterion of being good stories in mind. They did, however, fill a significant gap in the market. Simplified versions of popular myths and legends appeared, making them more accessible to teachers as well as children. Perhaps the area that received the greatest interest was children's fiction and how it could promote historical learning. Existing stories were reassessed for their historical potential. In addition, there was a notable increase of high-quality picture books which provide teachers with texts and illustrations that help promote learning in history. Many stand the test of re-reading to and by children: indeed, some could be described as modern classics of their type. Thus concepts such as change could be explored through stories such as *Jack's Basket* (Catley 1989).

Dora's Book (Edwards 1990) and *The Sandal* (Bradman and Dupasquier 1989) help children understand how different types of evidence are produced. *Once There Were Giants* (Waddell and Dale 1989), *Minny and Ginger* (Smith 1990) and *Our House* (Rogers and Rogers 1991) provide opportunities for discussing chronology and the passing of time. Children could be introduced to aspects of the past beyond living memory (Area of Study 1b) through books such as *Jack at Sea* (Dupasquier 1986), *Sir Cedric* (Gerrard 1988), and *The First Voyage of Christopher Columbus 1492* (Smith 1992). Teachers working in Key Stage 1 have become increasing skilful in drawing out the history potential of such texts, and in a review of inspection evidence in the early years of implementing the National Curriculum OFSTED drew attention to the successful use of story: 'Listening to and discussing stories promoted worthwhile historical learning' (OFSTED 1993: 6).

At Key Stage 2 there was a similar reassessment of existing works of historical fiction and an increase in the range of new historical fiction, with more provision appropriate to younger pupils and less confident readers. Again, the commissioning of authors resulted in examples of texts linked closely to the units contained within the programme of study. Anglia Young Books built up a series which included additional support packs of resources to extend use of the story (Childs 1991; Barnard 1992). In the 'Quick Read' series, below-average readers were provided with access to history stories related to specific Key Stage 2 study units.

The 1995 revised orders

In the light of such as positive response to the use of fiction at both Key Stages, the Dearing review's reduction in the prominence of story was therefore greeted with some surprise. This was especially so at Key Stage 1, where teachers noted that story received a much lower priority than previously in the history programme of study. Specific references appeared in Key Element 2a: 'Range and depth of historical knowledge and understanding' where pupils should be taught 'about periods of the past through stories from different periods and cultures, including stories and eyewitness accounts of historical events' (DfE 1995: 75).

Level Description 1 expressed expectations that children 'know and recount episodes from stories about the past.' (DfE 1995: 82) However, specific references were absent and the guidance provided in the earlier version of the National Curriculum was omitted. In Key Stage 2 the picture was bleaker, with no direct references to story or historical fiction within the revised programme of study. The reduction in emphasis had implications for teaching history. Primary teachers who taught through the curriculum changes since 1991 will be better able to flesh out the very bare bones of the current model. Thus they will be in a position to draw on prior experience of using picture books and historical fiction at Key Stages 1 and 2 respectively, to promote historical knowledge, concepts and skills in line with National Curriculum requirements. Others, particularly non-specialists, who have worked only with the current orders may lack the knowledge and understanding to develop activities based on fiction as part of their history topic or study unit. Over time this may result in a narrowing of the experiences offered to children.

Working with story at Key Stage 1

The focus for work with children was the potential of fiction to convey aspects of knowledge about the distant past. Area of Study 1a requires that children investigate 'aspects of the way of life of people in Britain in the past beyond living memory' (DfE 1995: 74). This involves going back beyond the time when the oldest people alive today were born. As the accepted life span is 100 years, this takes us back to pre-1897. However, the choice of precisely which time in the past is left open to teachers. Areas of Study 2 (famous people) has received particular attention from publishers. For example, Tutankhamun, Mary Seacole, Boudicca and Alfred the Great appeared in simple story books published by Ginn. Famous events (Area of Study 3) have also been the subject of stories: for example, *The Voyage of the Mayflower*

(Mitchelhill 1991) and *The Great Plague* (Vicary 1993). However, inspection findings gathered over the last five years indicate that the teaching of the past beyond living memory is a weak element in a fairly positive overall picture of history teaching at Key Stage 1 (OFSTED 1996). Projects investigating life eighty or ninety years ago are much in evidence but there seems to be some reluctance among many teachers to go back further into the past. There are several reasons for this situation, not least of which are a lack of teacher subject knowledge and the limited availability of resources that are appropriate for younger pupils. Not surprisingly, this part of the Key Stage 1 programme of study has been identified as requiring attention: 'In Key Stage 1 schools need to broaden their approach to history, in particular by giving more attention to more distant places and times' (OFSTED 1996: 15).

Thus teachers need to consider how they plan for and support children's knowledge of the past beyond living memory. This is where story comes into its own, because many of the non-fiction texts depicting the distant past are inappropriate for the learning needs of this age group. Stories are a particularly valuable resource for teachers who wish to introduce their pupils to a time in the distant past. Stories are adaptable and can be used to greater or lesser depth depending on the content. A picture book set in the past beyond living memory can be read to children during story time with follow-up confined to a discussion about the historical elements of the story and illustrations. An example such as *The Flyaway Pantaloons* (Scullard 1988), set in medieval Italy, could be used in this way. At the other extreme, the story can provide the context for a programme of historical activities lasting over several lessons which develop children's knowledge of a distant time in the past.

The story *Seeing Red* (Garland 1996) was selected for use with a mixed ability group of year 2 children. There were several reasons for this choice. First, it is not part of a specially commissioned history series, but a children's picture book set in the past. Thus it has an extended story-line and large format. *Seeing Red* is set during a recognisable period, the Napoleonic Wars of the early 1800s – well beyond living memory – and is based on a supposedly real event. Thus it can be classed as a legend, albeit a fairly recent one, as it has 'a grain of historical truth' (Maddern 1992). In addition, the narrative introduces Napoleon Bonaparte, a real person (though one with whom the children are unlikely to be familiar). The story has a strong narrative structure, with a clear beginning, middle and end. Furthermore, the plot centres on a strong female character, Trewenna. It is presented in the form of a picture book with illustrations provided by the well-established artist Tony Ross. His illustrations are full of life and humour and with a style very different from those produced to accompany the child-level texts of some commercial sets. As will be seen, they do raise interesting issues when viewed in the context of their potential for conveying historical knowledge. The story is set in a Cornish village which is saved from a French invasion by a small girl, Trewenna, who persuades the women to hide in the bushes on the cliff top and show their red petticoats. The French soldiers mistake the flashes of red they see for English redcoat soldiers lying in ambush and so return to their warships without firing a shot. Napoleon Bonaparte orders his invasion fleet back to France and Trewenna is a heroine. The main aims were to find out on a basic level what children understood of the story, whether they were aware of its historical element, how they interpreted the illustrations and whether the story could be used productively as a context for activities which were history focused but developed children's language skills.

Seeing Red is a more complex story than would at first appear. Consequently it was necessary to read it more than once in order to fix the key characters, events and their order in the children's minds. During the initial reading, the narrative had to be interrupted by the need to explain unfamiliar historical vocabulary such as warship, musket and flintlock pistols. At this point simple verbal explanations were given in order to maintain the flow of the story and with the knowledge that follow-up activities would take place which would clarify children's understanding. However, the meaning of 'redcoat' required a fuller explanation since a clear understanding was essential if children were to fully appreciate the link between the red of the women's petticoats and the uniforms worn by English soldiers at that time. At this point reference to source material was made. The group looked at a reproduction of a watercolour depicting a soldier of the time wearing the clothes that earned the nickname 'redcoat'. One child made an immediate link to the dress uniforms of modern soldiers worn during ceremonial occasions and seen on television.

Re-reading the story provided opportunities to clarify the chronology of the events in the children's minds. We then moved on to explore their interpretation of what they were seeing and hearing. The children were quick to agree that this was a story about 'the olden days' – though precisely how long ago was open to debate with suggestions varying from ninety years ago to 'hundreds of years ago'. The reasons given were the clues in the illustrations – the clothes worn, the design of the warships, the weapons shown, objects such as a candlestick and bellows, and the vocabulary. When asked about what parts of the story, if any, could have really happened, most of the children decided that all the events could have taken place. The only exceptions given were the dog and cat wearing red socks (p. 4), which they explained as a product of the illustrator's sense of humour. It became clear, however, that the impressionistic, fairytale style of the illustrations was misleading some children. One child decided that the story could not be true because ' the people don't look real'. At this point a copy of a portrait of Napoleon Bonaparte was used to introduce the children to the idea that 'Old Boney' was a real person. The idea of a nickname being used was not problematic to the children – probably as a result of their experiences in school and at home. They described it as 'a skitting name' and the aim was 'to make everyone laugh at him.' Further discussion took place about the fact that France and England were at war with each other 200 years ago and that the story was based on something that is supposed to have happened.

Using photocopies of six illustrations for a group sequencing activity, each child took it in turn to retell a section of the story in his or her own words, explaining what happened and why. The children demonstrated a good grasp of the key points, apart from one child who could not understand why the French soldiers ran away when they had guns and swords to fight with. This idea of motivation, of why people in the past acted as they did, was explored further in the context of why 'Old Boney' wanted to bring his soldiers to England. Reasons given included:

He didn't like the English.
He wanted to have power.
He wanted to be king of England.
He wanted to take land.
He wanted to catch English soldiers and make them fight for him.
He wanted to get hold of money.

In view of their lack of historical knowledge about the period the children's suggestions indicate a surprisingly sophisticated awareness of what motives often lie behind conflicts. The children may have used understanding gained from watching media news reports of modern wars to explain the motives of 'Old Boney'. There was also evidence that they had applied ideas gained through earlier discussion of motivation and power during a drama workshop based on the legend of King Midas. The notion of empathy was explored further through an activity which required the children, after observation and discussion, to imagine they were a character in one of the illustrations and record what they could see, hear and smell and what their feelings were in that situation. One child, imagining he was one of the French soldiers sailing in a rowing boat on a rough sea towards the shore wrote:

I am a French soldier.

I can see	**I can hear**
the sailors rowing	the sea whooshing
white waves	the oars ploshing in the water
the grey sky	the wind blowing
other soldiers looking scared	someone being sick
the warships	

I can smell	I feel
the sea	very excited
the sick	scared
	a little bit poorly

What was learnt

This small-scale project suggests a number of tentative conclusions about using picture storybooks set in the past beyond living memory:

- The importance of context is crucial and this requires background information for the teacher. Some authors do this (Manson 1990; Wildsmith 1995). The inclusion of a paragraph in *Seeing Red* giving basic information about when the Napoleonic Wars took place and a simple explanation of why a French fleet was sent to England would help teachers' preparation for reading the book. To some extent it would highlight that this story is more complex than would first appear. Additional details of where the story is believed to have taken place would be useful.
- It is important that teachers clarify the historical aspects with the children. This may range from a simple explanation that a story is set against a background of a specific time in the past to more detailed clarification of specific historical events or personalities.
- The use of unfamiliar historical vocabulary, if excessive, can get in the way of the story. Verbal explanations are inadequate when children do not have sufficient background knowledge of the time depicted to draw on. Some stories may fit more appropriately part way through a history topic instead of providing an initial stimulus to a project.
- A story of this type must be supported by source material if the historical potential is to be developed. Without this, children just assume the story is about another place and time, akin to fairy stories or space adventures.
- The illustrative style needs to be considered as it can influence children's perceptions of whether a story has elements that are made up or is true.
- Children are more able to discuss difficult and unfamiliar ideas through the story context.
- A story like *Seeing Red* can stimulate interest and curiosity, raising historical questions which require further research in order to find answers. In finding answers children increase their knowledge of a particular period.
- The follow-up activities provide many opportunities for the children to develop their listening, speaking, reading and writing. With more time this could be extended, Table 6.1 sets out suggestions for activities which support English as well as history.

Table 6.1 Examples of story-based activities which link history and English

Activity	History links	English links
1 Sequence pictures of key events in the story. Retell the story	Placing events in chronological order. Use terms linked to passing of time	Story structure and setting. Comparison of oral and written versions
2 Create picture dictionary of historical vocabulary. Use non-fiction books and sources	Use historical terms. Acquisition of knowledge. Historical enquiry	Understand what a dictionary is for. Alphabetical order. Definitions
3 Put yourself in an illustration, discuss what you see, hear, smell, feel	Empathy. Use historical vocabulary. Interpretation	Features of characters. Aspects of setting (place and time)
4 Research aspects of daily life in 1800. Use sources and non-fiction books	Historical enquiry. Asking questions. Use of sources. Historical knowledge	Select appropriate non-fiction books, use index. Difference between fiction and non-fiction texts
5 Compare Trewenna's life with the life of a modern child (chart form)	Knowledge of the period. Similarities and differences. Communication	Note taking. Understand different ways of conveying information
6 Discuss motivation of different characters and their actions. Record using speech bubbles	Recognise why people acted as they did, consequences	Reasons for events. Influence of setting on behaviour. Use text vocabulary
7 Retell story from another character's point of view	Chronology of events. Motivation. Interpretation of events	Character profiles. Plot (alternatives). Speculating what might have happened if . . .
8 Compare a redcoat with a modern soldier (labelled drawing)	Similarities/differences. Continuity/change. Historical knowledge	Use new vocabulary. Using labels to convey information.
9 Read *Jack at Sea* (Dupasquier 1987) and compare (set in same period)	Comparison of two interpretations	Compare theme, setting, characters, plot, events, illustrations

Developing the use of story at Key Stage 2

The value of history stories for older pupils is long established, to a greater extent than with younger children. Much of the rationale providing support for the inclusion of history stories in the Key Stage 1 history curriculum is equally applicable to Key Stage 2 (Blyth and Hughes 1997). In a further development of the publishing trends observed in Key Stage 1, the 'traditional' form of historical fiction (in which the text often stood alone) has been augmented by the production of picture books designed for older pupils in which the historical stories are accompanied by illustrations, often of a very high quality. For many pupils the visual images may be the initial point of contact, encouraging them to choose the book to read in the first place. Two good examples are *Pepi and the Secret Names* (Paton Walsh and French 1996) and *The Winged Cat* (Nourse Lattimore 1992). Both stories provide information about beliefs, rituals and ways of life in Ancient Egypt. The texts are accompanied by beautiful illustrations that are clearly based on original source material from the time, and indeed, in the second example, the author provides information about her sources. Thus pupils are provided with a model for the process of illustrating their own history stories, using sources to ensure accuracy.

It is worth noting that the value of historical fiction can extend beyond the bounds of the subject discipline and, depending on the content, it can help to promote the spiritual, moral, social and cultural dimensions (SMSC) of older primary pupils' understanding. This use of historical fiction can be extended by developing a literature theme using historical fiction set in different periods. In this way pupils could examine recurring topics such as the search for freedom, the movement of peoples and the human cost of war. *When Hitler Stole Pink Rabbit* (Kerr 1993) looks at life in Nazi Germany, escape and living as a refugee in wartime Britain. *The Silver Sword* (Serraillier 1956) presents another picture of children's experience of war through the travels of a group of refugee children who are searching for their father in Europe. A book such as *The Discus Thrower* (Oakden 1992) can promote SMSC by not only informing its readers about life in Ancient Greece, but also by raising questions about the roles of different groups such as children, women and slaves and by encouraging pupils to reflect and think critically about issues. A good historical narrative forces examination of these issues because the story cannot work without an understanding of different constraints on characters within it. This is in stark contrast to the 'costume drama' category of historical fiction in which the period setting serves only as a backdrop for actions and events that could take place at any time.

Author studies on prolific writers such as Robert Westall and Jill Paton Walsh give pupils a chance to research one creator of historical fiction in greater depth and examine ways in which stories are created from facts. One approach is to gather together as many books as possible by the author and, after reading and rereading, decide how the books are connected. Robert Westall based many of his stories on home life during the Second World War and often used a newspaper report as a starting point for historical fiction. Drawing on his personal experiences and primary source material he creates vivid and detailed pictures of wartime Britain (Westall 1975). Biography often bridges the gap between historical fiction and information books. A life story might read like fiction but, as with non-fiction texts, it will be based on facts which can be documented. In the past, biography written for children used more fictional techniques than those written for adults. The current trend is for greater authenticity and thus biographies frequently use primary source materials such as letters and photographs to provide the visual evidence for the story.

Many authors of historical novels, like Robert Westall, have been attracted to and have focused on particular historical periods. Rosemary Sutcliff and Henry Treece set many of their historical stories in the distant past of the Romans, Anglo-Saxons and Vikings. However, their books do not always make easy reading, even for proficient readers at the top end of the primary school. These texts are, however, excellent for reading aloud and there have been several adaptations produced for television and radio. Reading aloud to older primary pupils tends to occur less frequently than in the past (Evans 1997). Reading aloud a piece of historical fiction which relates to the history topic provides access to this genre for those pupils whose reading skills would not support independent reading of the book. The teacher also provides a model which can encourage pupils to choose to read this particular genre. Huck *et al.* (1995) noted that historical fiction is not as popular amongst primary pupils as it was a generation ago, despite the increase in texts available, many of which are set at a more appropriate level than hitherto. The use of historical fiction for both history and English activities can reverse this trend, as children often cite texts that have been read aloud to them by their teachers as among their favourite books (Millard 1997). Table 6.2 illustrates how, in a project on Ancient Greece, activities linked to a text such as *In the Lap of Athena* (Goddard 1995) can be used to support both English and history teaching. The story is written in the form of a diary with the Battle of Salamis providing the historical setting.

Looking ahead

At the time of writing the status of all foundation subjects is endangered by the concern to raise literacy and numeracy standards. The National Literacy Strategy (NLS) has potentially wide-reaching implications for the place of history stories and historical fiction. In Key Stage 1 it is suggested that reception children are introduced to traditional stories, with the range extending to familiar settings and fantasy worlds in year 1. Stories from other cultures appear in year 2, term 2. There is no specific reference in the NLS

Table 6.2 Examples of story-based activities which link the history of Ancient Greece and English

Activity	History links	English links
1 Devise a time line to illustrate key historical events mentioned in the story	The ability to place events within a chronological framework	Locating story events in real historical time. Explore narrative orders by identifying and mapping out sequences of events in stories
2 Identify and record factual information provided in the story about aspects of daily life in ancient Greece in the fifth century BC	Acquire knowledge and understanding about daily life in ancient Greece	Investigate settings and explore clues in the text about everyday lives
3 Use non-fiction sources such as reference books, photographs of artefacts, buildings and sites and CD-Roms to cross-check reliability of the evidence collected about daily life	Use primary and secondary source material to enquire about daily life in ancient Greece	Use study skills in the use of information texts and visual evidence to cross-check some of the facts
4 Identify and record characteristic features of the period which the story illustrates, such as the position of women, children and slaves	Gain knowledge and understanding about the life experiences of different groups in ancient Greece	Identify the way in which particular characteristics of the society influence the way in which the characters can act and the narrative can be told
5 Identify and record differences between the lives of children in the story and the lives of children today	Recall, select and organise historical information; communicate knowledge and understanding of the period	Speculate about the consequences for characters' behaviour in relation to the story

to stories set in the past at Key Stage 1 and this may lead to neglect of this category of fiction. The omission continues to Key Stage 2. The use of story is specified for year 4, when it is suggested that pupils spend term 1 focusing on historical stories, short novels and play scripts (DfEE 1998). In year 6, term 2, pupils may work with historical stories and novels as one of a range of genres. In addition to the literacy content specified in the National Literacy Framework (ibid.), historical stories could be used as the context for activities with a history focus. Pupils could be involved in:

- investigating the settings and exploring clues about everyday lives, clothes, artefacts, transport and details on locations;
- locating the story events in 'real historical time';
- making the distinction between fact and fiction;
- using non-fiction texts to cross-check evidence;
- using historical stories as models for writing: this might involve retelling incidents in the story from a particular character's point of view and linking their own experience to historical stories.

This approach to historical stories, specifically fiction, has some very real dangers if this genre is to be reduced to a term's work within an hour's focus on literacy. Margaret Meek (1996) provides some challenging thoughts about the current sharp distinction made between information texts and fiction. She notes the assumption made by writers such as Neate (1992) that children move on from narrative to informational texts – with the implication that non-fiction is in some way superior to fiction. In questioning whether pupils have to leave behind accounts of the world which are fictional in order to acquire knowledge she comments:

> There is no step-by-step way through the world of facts. Instead readers turn to new voices telling them things in different kinds of language . . . from all kinds of texts, narrative or non-narrative.
>
> (Meek 1996: 25)

This should be an ongoing process – with pupils having access to history stories of different types throughout their school life. Children's texts produced for different reading levels, picture books set in the past, historical fiction read aloud to the class can all make a contribution to pupils' under-standing and images of past times. It is a naive and worrying assumption to regard the genre as only appropriate at one particular stage of learning and then to limit its use further to a specific year group as part of their English programme (DfEE 1998). The current focus on literacy and numeracy has major implications for the primary curriculum, with calls to reduce the breadth of the current curriculum model in order to extend time for the 'basics', at least in the short term. Using history stories as a context for research, using sources, asking historical questions and acquiring knowledge of the past may offer one way in which history, at both key stages, can 'infiltrate' curriculum time allocated to English and literacy.

References

Teachers' books

Blyth, J. and Hughes, P. (1997) *Using Written Sources in Primary History*, London: Hodder and Stoughton.

Claire, H. (1996) *Reclaiming Our Pasts*, Stoke-on-Trent: Trentham Books.

Cox, K. and Hughes, P. (1990) *Early Years History: An Approach Through Story*, Liverpool: Liverpool Institute of Higher Education.

Department for Education (DfE) (1995) *Key Stages 1 and 2 of the National Curriculum*, London: HMSO.

Department for Education and Employment (DfEE) (1998) *National Literacy Strategy Framework for Teaching*, London: DfEE.

Department of Education and Science (DES) (1990) *National Curriculum History Working Group Final Report*, London: HMSO.

—— (1991a) *History in the National Curriculum*, London: HMSO.

—— (1991b) *Non-statutory Guidance for History in the National Curriculum*, York: National Curriculum Council.

Evans, J. (1997) 'The Storytime Session: a Dying Art Worthy of Revival?', *Language and Learning*, 29–31.

Gadsden, A. (1991) *Geography and History Through Stories: Key Stage 1*, Sheffield: Geographical Association.

Huck, C., Hepler, F. and Hickman, J. (1995) *Children's Literature*, New York: Harcourt Brace Jovanovich.

Husbands, C. (1996) *What is History Teaching?*, Buckingham: Open University Press.

Little, V. and John, T. (1986) *Historical Fiction in the Classroom*, London: Historical Association.

Maddern, E. (1992) *A Teacher's Guide to Storytelling at Historic Sites*, Colchester, Essex: English Heritage.

Meek, M. (1996) *Information and Book Learning*, Stroud, Glos.: Thimble Press.

Millard, E. (1997) *Differently Literate*, London: Falmer.

National Curriculum Council (NCC) (1993) *Teaching History at Key Stage One*, York: NCC.

Neate, B. (1992) *Finding Out about Finding Out*, London: Hodder and Stoughton.

Office for Standards in Education (OFSTED) (1993) *History Key Stages 1, 2 and 3 Second Year, 1992–93*, London: HMSO.

—— (1996) *Subjects and Standards: Issues for School Development Arising from OFSTED Inspection findings 1994–5*, London: HMSO.

Children's books

Ahlberg, J. and A. (1981) *Peepo*, Harmondsworth, Middx: Puffin Books.

Barnard, P. (1992) *Escape from the Workhouse*, Saffron Walden, Essex: Anglia Young Books.

Benjamin, A. (1996) *Young Rosa Parks*, USA: Troll Associates.

Bradman, T. and Dupasquier, P. (1989) *The Sandal*, London: Andersen Press.

Catly, A. (1989) *Jack's Basket*, London: Beaver Books.

Childs, A. (1991) *Under the Rose*, Saffron Walden, Essex: Anglia Young Books.

Dupasquier, P. (1987) *Jack at Sea*, Harmondsworth, Middx: Puffin Books.

Edwards, M. (1990) *Dora's Book*, Minneapolis: Carolrhoda Books.

Garland, S. (1996) *Seeing Red*, London: Andersen Press.

Gerrard, R. (1988) *Sir Cedric*, London: Lynx.

Goddard, G. (1995) *In the Lap of Athena*, Leamington Spa, War.: Scholastic.

Kerr, J. (1993) *When Hitler Stole Pink Rabbit*, London: HarperCollins.

Manson, C. (1990) *Two Travellers*, London: Walker Books.

Mitchelhill, B. (1991) *The Mayflower*, Aylesbury, Bucks: Ginn.

Nourse Lattimore, D. (1992) *The Winged Cat*, London: HarperCollins.

Oakden, D. (1992) *The Discus Thrower*, Saffron Walden, Essex: Anglia Young Books.

Paton Walsh, J. and French, F. (1996) Pepi and the Secret Names, London: Frances Lincoln.

Potter, T. (1996) *Louis Braille*, London: Franklin Watts.

Rogers, E. and Rogers, P. (1991) *Our House*, London: Walker Books.

Scullard, S. (1988) *The Flyaway Pantaloons*, London: Pan Macmillan Children's Books.

Serraillier, I. (1956) *The Silver Sword*, Harmondsworth, Middx: Puffin Books.

Smith, B. (1990) *Minny and Ginger*, London: Pavilion Books.

—— (1992) *The First Voyage of Christopher Columbus 1492*, Harmondsworth, Middx: Puffin Books.

Vicary, T. (1993) *The Great Plague*, Oxford: Oxford University Press.

Waddell, M. & Dale, P. (1989) *Once There were Giants*, London: Walker Books.

Westall, R. (1975) *The Machine Gunners*, London: Puffin Books.

Wildsmith, B. (1995) *Saint Francis*, Oxford: Oxford University Press.

7

CHILDREN'S AWARENESS OF TIME IN STORY AND HISTORICAL FICTION

Pat Hoodless

Language is a major vehicle for studying children's understanding of such an abstract notion as time. If we listen to children talking we can begin to make some assumptions about what they know and how their language develops. This chapter gives an account of some classroom activities devised as a means of investigating primary children's understanding of time and chronology and also development of their use of the language of time. Books and stories were used to encourage children to talk about history, time and chronology as they perceived it and the discussions were recorded and analysed for evidence of language use about time and chronology.

Most teachers would agree that time is, indeed, a very complex concept, particularly for children. There are many ways of perceiving time, depending very much on how we experience it. However, what seems to be a significant distinction to make about time, in relation to children's learning, is that awareness of time and chronology *as children experience them* is a very different learning experience from trying to grasp the conventions of *time measurement*. I propose in this chapter that children of primary school age do, in fact, have quite sophisticated understandings of time, but find the conventions of measuring it, for a number of reasons, much more difficult to master.

Past research

Past research into children's understanding of time falls fairly distinctly into two types: early research, which was characterised by statistical analysis; and later research, which relied more on qualitative methods – what children said and did, and the influence of the context on this, rather than simply how many children gave the correct response to a question. From the 1920s until the 1970s research was influenced by the maturational theory of Piaget; it suggested that children's skill and understanding of time was not generally acquired until about the age of fourteen or fifteen. Subsequent early research, such as that reported in an article by Jahoda (1963) was dominated by quantitative methods. It tended to corroborate such findings and did little to challenge this established view. Early research findings, however, were appropriate to teaching contexts at that time and cannot necessarily be applied to present-day children or to current approaches to primary teaching.

Since the 1970s and 1980s, however, the scope of research has broadened and, with it, new attitudes towards children's capabilities have emerged. In the field of educational psychology, Paul Fraisse (1982) argues that children and adults make use of the same information processing skills in their experiences of time, and that the differences between the capabilities of the child and the adult are not as fundamental as Piaget suggested. Children are simply less able to analyse the multiple data of experience and to establish the relations between changes. Others such as William Friedman (1982) have also focused on the qualitative nature of children's understanding. He argues that statistical research based on activities such as ordering cards actually tells us very little about the processes which underlie those performances. It is the reasoning behind the child's actions and words which is significant.

Recent studies undertaken by historians have reflected this shift in emphasis towards qualitative analysis, where the child's responses are recorded in a familiar context, while carrying out meaningful tasks. John West (1981) is convinced that children do develop a sense of time throughout their primary school years. He has found that young children can sequence artefacts and pictures accurately, often using historical knowledge acquired outside school. He argues that it is merely a 'numerical' sense of time that they find difficult. Instead, teachers should capitalise on what children *can* do, such as developing their sense of contemporaneity and their skill in 'time-placing'. Joan Blyth (1994) has found that children can sequence pictures accurately if the number of pictures is carefully controlled, depending on the child's maturity.

Linda Levstik (Levstik and Pappas 1987), investigating children's responses to historical narratives, argues that traditional investigations have failed to take sufficient account of the effect of context on understanding, especially the forms of discourse used. Hilary Cooper's (1992) research into primary history suggests that there is a pattern in the development of concepts, including temporal ones, which need to be taught and are best learned through discussion. The belief that direct, structured teaching fosters the acquisition of time concepts and related language is reiterated in a number of recent research articles and publications (see, for example, Hoodless 1996).

What do children say about time?

Children inadvertently reveal a great deal about their awareness of time and chronology when talking about what they can remember or know about history or the past. Students working on their BEd history course at Didsbury School of Education in Manchester recorded children's responses to very straightforward, direct questions, such as 'What is history?', or 'What do you know about the past?' These questions were asked of children of all ages and abilities, in order to make a comparison between the groups questioned.

In one school, children aged four and five tended to give one-word answers of a very concrete nature, showing a hazy idea of what 'history' means, and apparently applying it to their general knowledge rather than to anything specific:

Teacher: Do you know what history is about?
B: Monster aliens.
K: Dinosaurs.
D: Tigers.

On the other hand, responses in a different school from children also aged four and five did indicate some understanding:

Teacher: Does anybody know what history is?
N: Is it about the past?
Ni: Is it college work?

In this example, in a school where there was a high level of interest in history, the children were from a middle-class, largely professional catchment area. More importantly, though, they first talked about things they had been doing the previous day, which had possibly alerted them to the general topic of conversation.

Children in year 2 classes were generally more aware of the meaning of the initial question and also had more detailed recollections of past events in their own lives. In addition to this, some used phrases and referred to the past in more general terms:

Teacher: What do you think history is about?
Ka: Before things really happened?
S: Old cars?
D: Old things and new things?

The children's continuing uncertainty here is reflected in the interrogative tone they all used in answering the question – they were seeking confirmation of their emerging thoughts. Despite this, they demonstrated marked progression from the younger groups.

By year 3, children of seven or eight years were talking in more abstract terms, finding appropriate language to voice three completely different perceptions of the past. They were clearly aware of the need to know more specific detail:

Teacher: What is history?
J: A subject?
J: Is it a long time ago?
G: It's an adventure.
Teacher: Can anyone tell me anything about history?
J: I don't know anything about history. My dad could tell you something about it.
G: Didn't they wear different types of clothes?
A: They built their houses with a lot of glass in them.
G: No they didn't. They were stick houses.
J: Yeh, they were made of wood.

Older children in years 4, 5 and 6 were generally talking in precise terms and in a more definite tone when asked about history:

Teacher: What is history?
J: Old things.
K: Things that happen in the past.
S: When you were younger.
(Year 4)

Teacher: What do you think history is about?
B: It's about things long ago.
A: Talking about things in the past.
C: Years and years ago.
(Year 5/6)

Teacher: What is history?
A: Looking back in the past.
M: Thinking about the past.
J Old things and people at war.
T: It's really good, to do with the past.
Teacher: Is history a long time ago or not?
J: It can be hundreds of years or just a few years.
M: Could be yesterday.
J: But some people may not think yesterday is interesting.
(Year 4)

In this last extract, children are actually entering into a debate about what part of the past can rightly be called history. A similar discussion occurred spontaneously in another class:

S: I don't think history *is* yesterday, only years ago.
K: History *is* yesterday.
J: No, history is a long time ago.

(Year 4)

These interesting debates arose from earlier conversations and were on one occasion a clear response to a more searching question, suggesting that the quality of the questioning used by teachers significantly influences the nature of children's responses. The debate itself stimulated considerable use of the language of time. In such a situation as this there is a wonderful opportunity for teachers to build on what children know and move them on in terms of their language use, to develop, for instance, terms such as the recent/distant past, early/modern history, modern/medieval/ancient times, and also to explore further what the term 'history' means. Obviously, the children are interested in these issues.

Frequently, it was the abstract use of dates and spans of time, involving calculation and measurement, which the children seemed to find most difficult:

Teacher: Do any old people talk to you about history?
J: My grandad was in the war. He's got war medals.
Teacher: How long ago was the war?
G: Either six or sixteen years ago.
J: Was it a thousand years ago?
A: A hundred years ago. My dad was in the army.

On the other hand, they could discuss with ease equally long spans of time in relation to their relatives' ages, even recognising the humour in the deliberate mistakes in their grandparents' jokes about their ages:

Teacher: Does anybody know how old their grandparents are?
J: Yes 50 or 60.
K: 70 or 80.
K: In their 40s.
S: Around 70.
K: My gran says she's 22!

Children in our samples began to remember history on a grander scale at around year 2, ages six and seven:

Ka: We have TV, they didn't. They did work. They just ate.
Ki: They had raggy clothes.
Ka: They had no cookers.
D: They had to cook it under the fire.

(Year 2)

Teacher: Does anybody know about any important things that have happened
in the past?
J: My great-great-grandad designed the penny black.
K: There has been two world wars.

(Year 4)

Teacher: What have you learned about history?
S: The history of Hazel Grove *(local area)*.
C: Yeh, we walked around the town and looked at old buildings.
Teacher: What words do you associate with history?
T: Greeks, exploration.
C: Egyptians.
S: Victorians.

(Year 6)

There is a progression here, from mainly social or personal history towards
a broader grasp of national history in different periods and there appears
to have been a significant impact on these children's knowledge from school
history lessons. This is reflected in the accurate use of historical terminology
to refer to the topics they had covered, including both historical periods and
broader trends such as exploration. These extracts suggest that children, even
in the pre-school years, bring with them a considerable knowledge of the
past, which broadens during their primary education. They also know about
the wide range of terms related to time and chronology, although their skill
in using this terminology can be limited, giving rise to inconsistencies and
inaccuracies in some contexts.

Sharing stories: children's fiction and historical fiction

The research in this section relates closely to current requirements of the
National Literacy Strategy (NLS) and both Key Stage 1 and Key Stage 2 (see
summaries of work in DfEE 1998: 66–7).

Story with early years and Key Stage 1

In order to see how children coped with the dimension of time in literature,
I shared with them stories such as *Come Away from the Water, Shirley*
(Burningham 1992) and *Where the Wild Things Are* (Sendak 1970). Both these
stories involve child characters who travel into imaginary time which
co-exists with the real, measured time of the adult world. In *Come Away from
the Water, Shirley*, John Burningham makes simultaneous use of two modes of
narration to tell the story of Shirley and her parents on a day's outing to the
beach. While the left-hand pages present the rather mundane day as it is
experienced by her parents, sitting on deckchairs, reading the paper and

having a nap, the right-hand pages are lively, full-colour pictures bringing us Shirley's imaginary adventures. Shirley passes through the day into the setting sun and darkness of night. She returns at the end of her adventure in bright moonlight, having spent a day and a night away. However, her parents have only been on the beach for two or three hours. Parallel times are also apparent in *Where the Wild Things Are*. Max travels into a dream world full of strange wild beasts. He is away on his adventure for many days and nights, but on his return to his bedroom it is still the same night and his supper is still hot. Evidently little 'real' time has passed.

After reading the stories with the children, discussions were initiated with a simple, open-ended question, such as: 'What do you think is happening in this story?' Most children seemed to understand the need to measure time accurately and to use appropriate terminology in doing so. Words to do with the measurement of time occurred throughout the conversations with children of all ages, although they were not always accurately used. Even the youngest referred to light and dark and night and day in estimating durations. Clock time was referred to spontaneously by some three- and four-year-old nursery children who attempted to be quite specific about the time of day in which the picture is set.

Measurement, in hours and minutes, featured more prominently in the talk of six- and seven-year-olds, some of whom tried to be very precise about their timings:

Teacher: How long do you think they were actually there, on the beach?
R: About two or three hours.
B: About two and a half hours.
C: Three hours.

These children were also aware that while her parents sat on the beach for only a few hours, Shirley, in her dream, was away for days and nights. They understood the significance of these terms as time markers, and were able to use them in an appropriate way.

Other children, talking about Shirley's adventure on the pirate ship, showed an emerging awareness of historical periods and chronological conventions:

Teacher: When did this happen, now or a long time ago?
N: A long time ago because of the boats, sail boats.
P: If it was now, there wouldn't be monsters now, monsters like dinosaurs.
N: Pirate boats.
P: There's no such thing as pirates. Well, there could of, millions and zillions of years ago.
Teacher: Could it happen today?
P: No.

P: It was about sixty years ago.

N: Treasure could be true, because there's gold under the ground. It could be true five days ago.

These children were aware that boats with sails belonged to a different age, and they introduced other incidental knowledge which revealed an incipient awareness of broad chronological distinctions. For example, they knew that dinosaurs belonged to a much earlier time, before the sailing boats. They also knew that treasure can be found now as well as in the time of the pirates, since it may still be under the ground. Not only are they revealing some awareness of chronological time here, but also a grasp of the key historical concepts of change and continuity. They know what has gone for good. They also know that other things may still exist and use simple, concrete ways of conveying this idea in language.

Some children's comments on *Come Away from the Water, Shirley* indicated a clear perception that 'experienced' time is different from 'real' time. This extract is from a discussion with six- and seven-year-olds:

Teacher: How long do you think Shirley's adventures seemed to go on for?

R: Quite a long time.

L: About a day because it was morning, and it shows you at night there – it's all dark, there it's not . . .

Teacher: So what seemed to happen to the time for Shirley?

L: It went longer.

R: It seems longer when you're imagining things.

P: Yes, like when you fall asleep, you think it's just a short time, but it's not.

L: And like in assembly, it feels a very long time.

These children have quite a well-developed understanding of how durations of time can appear to vary, depending upon how they are experienced. Time seems longer if you are day-dreaming, imagining things or sitting in a school assembly! These perceptions arose quite spontaneously, despite the fact that children of this age characteristically have difficulty with conventional clock time. Throughout the discussions, most children perceived the *need* to refer to time measurement and to chronology and to use specific terminology when doing so, even at a very early age. Their skill in doing this accurately remained limited until after the age of seven, however.

Stories which make use of time as a device are certainly an excellent stimulus and a good resource for extending children's understanding. Their potential needs to be fully exploited in the classroom, encouraging children to think carefully about what is happening in the story. Teachers need to focus on discussing the time dimension in the stories, since this was not a feature to which children naturally referred. In some groups, I found that discussion of time was not initiated until I intentionally focused attention on it through questioning.

The nature of the questioning was a significant factor in what was said. If questions were limited to 'How long?', or 'How much time passed?', then answers were similarly limited to this frame of reference. However, once I introduced the word 'seem' into the questioning, several children revealed the full range of their perceptions, at a more sophisticated level. We also need to consider how to extend to others the high level of perception held by a few children. This appears to have been a natural process in the course of discussion in two of my groups. Once one child commented on how long something seemed to last, others quickly gave their examples of the same phenomenon. Small group discussion, with carefully planned teacher interventions, certainly seems to be an effective means of raising both the quality of language use and also the perception of young children about time.

Using historical fiction at Key Stage 2

Children in years 4, 5 and 6 classes were asked to read some short stories about the Romans from *The Capricorn Bracelet*, by Rosemary Sutcliff (1990). Each chapter in *The Capricorn Bracelet* comprises a short story in its own right. They are set at different points in time during the Roman occupation of Britain but linked through the device of the bracelet, which is passed from generation to generation in each story. Rosemary Sutcliff, writing some time ago (*The Capricorn Bracelet* was first published in 1973), provides challenging reading for today's children, using her detailed historical research to produce text at a high level.

I worked with two groups of children in a school with a mixed intake containing children of a wide ability range. However, the more able readers were selected for this task, due partly to the short time available to us and partly to the level of reading difficulty involved. The first group of children had just completed work on the Study Unit 'Romans, Anglo-Saxons and Vikings in Britain' (DfE 1995) and knew a considerable amount of factual detail, which they used well in their interpretation of the book.

The first point to emerge was the children's awareness of the dates. A particular feature of this set of stories is the way in which the reader's attention is specifically drawn to the chronology. My first question was about the clues which someone might use who did not know the stories were about Roman times. The years 3 and 4 children referred to the picture on the front cover at first. I then drew their attention to the title of the first story, 'Death of a City AD 61' (Sutcliff 1990: 12):

Teacher: What about the title?
O: You can tell it's a long time ago because it's only 61.

P: You can guess why they're Romans, because they wear red clothes and they've got armour and spears.

N: How come they called London that?

P: Because they speak differently.

Teacher: What did they speak?

Ps: (*several*) Latin.

Teacher: How long do you think it is between the first story and the second story? How much time had gone by, do you think?

P: About two years?

O: Five?

Teacher: How could you work it out?

P: You could put that one . . .

N: The chapters are called 61 AD then one million and twenty three.

Although the problem of calculating the time spans accurately was not fully resolved, it is evident that one child was aware that the dates were significant and that one was later than the other. Another child, who was interrupted, was beginning to see a way of calculating the time span between the two dates. The children needed, however, to have their attention drawn specifically to these features, for although the whole volume made the chronology of the period a feature the children did not refer to it spontaneously as they did to other aspects, such as the illustrations. They also needed to be encouraged to go beyond their initial attempts using guesswork.

I drew their attention to the chronology using another chapter:

Teacher: What do you think that means, AD 383?

P: Anni Domini

N: No Anno Domini (*in unison*) three hundred and eighty three . . . thousand.

They were clearly still unsure of large numbers and possibly thought that a date must involve thousands somehow. Guesswork was widely used when they were asked detailed questions about spans of time:

Teacher: How long did the Romans stay in Britain?

P: Two years.

N: Twenty years.

Teacher: Longer than that.

O: A thousand.

Teacher: Well it was about four hundred years.

P: Ooh, that's a long time.

The problem here seems not to have been their knowledge and understanding of the period (they noticed details such as language, religious practices and dress, which placed the story in Roman times) but their inability to carry out numerical calculations.

Year 5 children were able to use confidently a wide range of 'clues' in their response to my initial question, revealing the depth of their knowledge about the period through their more highly developed use of vocabulary:

Teacher: When do you think it all happened?
S: I think it was in Roman times.
Teacher: Why did you think that?
S: Ancient Roman times, well, some of the language and the names, well, you know what I mean? They had, like, these walls.
K: The date's at the top.
Teacher: What does it mean? AD 61.
S: Anno Domini.
Teacher: Good. What language do you think that is?
S: Latin. (*explanation*)
Teacher: When would that be?
M: Sixty one years after Christ, and the other one's AD 383.

The children in year 5 also noticed how the bracelet appears in all the stories, connecting them even though they span a considerable length of time.

One child in particular was interested in a feature of the author's style. He commented on how the story often jumped from one point in time to another, apparently without warning:

M: Some of the time when I was reading it, it went to one part, straight to another [*sic*]. It might have been just the way I was reading it.
Teacher: Yes, it jumped about. Can you find the place where it does this?
M: It did it quite a few times. I thought it made the story hard to follow. Here there's an old man who says a few things at the beginning and then it doesn't tell you what's happening, it goes to something where they move on into the . . . It doesn't explain things and tell you when he's finished it just . . . He just explains a few things and then moves away.
Teacher: How do you know when the story has jumped?
D: It says 'Many months'.
M: Sometimes it doesn't do that, it just jumps to another thing.
S: It's like on TV it does that.
M: TV's a bit similar because you're watching it and you can take it all in.
S: But that's easier to follow, because you can see it all happening in front of you. You know what it looks like.
D: In TV you can make it go from house to house instead of like months or years. You can't really do that in here.

M: In one programme I saw, there was a baby, then he was like a kid, then he was in his teens and then he was grown up.

Although this was probably not intended to be a feature of the book, this child (M) picked up an interesting point about narrative writing in general: the way in which time is used in an arbitrary way to enable the author to move quickly from one event to another, or to create dramatic effect. He had noticed that narratives are not necessarily sequenced according to chronological time: 'it just jumps to another thing'. Once this kind of discussion had been initiated by one child, it was quickly picked up by the others in the group, who revealed their own awareness of the manipulation of time in other contexts such as TV and film. Here, the children were demonstrating their prior awareness that authors can make use of time to suit their own purpose, an important link with literacy. What was interesting, however, was that they had made this initial discovery through watching TV and film, while still finding it difficult to deal with in reading.

The same child was also quite critical of the book's style. He felt that the stories were too predictable and not exciting enough for modern children. Others agreed with his opinions:

M: You'd cry, wouldn't you if someone like your sister has died and in here it says, the man came to the door and told them, and it was like, right then, see yer.
Teacher: Well this author began writing some time ago, and in those days, writers might have been anxious not to upset child readers.
M: But you like a bit of excitement and adventure, don't you?
S: Yes, like in Roald Dahl's books.
M: This isn't really a very good story for children because children now, they wouldn't want to read all this. They like to read more exciting ones.
S: I think if they made it more modern then it would be an interesting story.

These ten-year-olds were aware that the book had been written some time ago and that styles of writing for children have changed. They quickly grasped the notion that they had read a story *written* in one time in the past but *about* another, more distant time in the past. They found this idea quite interesting, probably because it was adding to their awareness of how reading and writing change over time.

What emerged from these enquiries was the fact that historical fiction tended to develop the children's detailed awareness of a particular historical period. These stories are fixed within a specific time frame rather than moving through time, thus providing less opportunity for explicit discussion of the concept. Each story did, however, contribute to the children's sense of contemporaneity and general 'feel' for an age in the past, in itself an important aspect of chronology, if this aspect of time is to have any meaning at all for children.

The device of setting each story at a different chronological time provided me with an opportunity to encourage the children to focus on the dates and to engage in some estimation and calculation of the spans of time involved in the book. With most of the children, and especially those below the age of ten, the dates needed to be pointed out, since they did not generally refer to them of their own accord. Nearly all of them found the use of dates and the numerical calculation involved in discussing periods of time very problematic.

As with the earlier books which used time as a device, *The Capricorn Bracelet* also gave rise to some discussion of how you can travel in time in a book, on the television or even in your head. It was exciting to see the children's realisation growing as they discussed how this is what you are having to do when you think about another time in the past; that historical study and reading stories about the past is, in fact, a kind of time travel, which we attempt using many different devices, not least our own minds.

References

Blyth, J. (1994) *History 5 to 11*, London: Hodder and Stoughton.

Burningham, J. (1992) *Come Away from the Water, Shirley*, London: Random Century Children's Books.

Cooper, H. (1992) *The Teaching of History*, London: Fulton.

Department for Education (DfE) (1995) *History in the National Curriculum*, London: HMSO.

Department for Education and Employment (DfEE) (1998) *The National Literacy Strategy Framework for Teaching*, London: DfEE.

Fraisse, P. (1982) 'The Adaptation of the Child to Time', in W.J. Friedman (ed.), *The Developmental Psychology of Time*, New York: Academic Press.

Friedman, W.J. (1982) *The Developmental Psychology of Time*, New York: Academic Press.

Hoodless, P. (1996) *Time and Timelines in the Primary School*, Teaching of History Series no. 69, London: Historical Association.

Jahoda, G. (1963) 'Children's Concepts of Time and History', *Educational Review*, 15: 87–104.

Levstik, L.S., and Pappas, C. (1987) 'Exploring the Development of Historical Understanding', *Journal of Research and Development in Education*, 21: 1–15.

Sendak, M. (1970) *Where the Wild Things Are*, Harmondsworth, Middx: Penguin.

Sutcliff, R. (1990) *The Capricorn Bracelet*, London: Random House Children's Books.

West, J. (1981) 'Time Charts', *Education 3–13*, 10,1: 48–50.

8

TEACHING READING SKILLS AND HISTORY AT KEY STAGE 2

A complementary approach

Julie Davies and Amanda Donoghue

Introduction

Reading matters; being able to read is both a means and an end to enhancing life both materially and intellectually. For this reason, it is considered by teachers, parents and society alike as a fundamentally important skill which should be taught systematically and rigorously throughout the primary years. There is increasing awareness that there is a disparity between the quality of teaching reading at Key Stage 1 compared to Key Stage 2. Information regarding reading standards, collected by OFSTED, was reported by Her Majesty's Chief Inspector thus:

> In over half of schools, pupils' reading skills are good in both key stages, but in just under one in ten in Key Stage 1, and one in eight at Key Stage 2 they are poor. Many pupils are not able to read accurately.
>
> (OFSTED 1997: 11)

This is a long-standing problem. The HMI report on the *Teaching and Learning of Reading in Primary Schools* (DES 1991: 1) states: 'In Key Stage 2 the children's reading skills and the range of their reading experiences were insufficiently extended in the majority of classes.' The report went on to say: 'Despite the satisfactory standards of fluency in many year 6 classes, less than half provided sufficient opportunities for pupils to reach much beyond level 4 of the National Curriculum or to develop the ability to read more critically' (ibid.: 6).

More particularly, 'throughout the various HMI survey reports of recent years, there are many suggestions that the possibilities for developing reading beyond the initial stages have not been fully recognised' (Beard 1994: 273). Dissatisfaction with reading standards at Key Stage 2 has led to several recent governmental initiatives. The Secretary of State for Education and Employment has set as the government's target the raising, within the next five years, from 57 per cent to 80 per cent of the number of year 6 children who will attain the expected standard, level 4 (Carvel 1997a). The introduction of national tests in reading at year 4 is expected to keep every-one's eye on the ball of reading standards throughout the junior years and to pick up those falling behind. Twelve literacy centres have been set up throughout the country (DfEE 1997). A major element in raising standards is a daily literacy hour in every classroom (Bright 1997). This innovation has received strong support from the National Association of Headteachers (NAHT) which stated that the time traditionally given to the teaching and learning of reading has been eroded over the last eight years (Carvel 1997b). The NAHT advocates decreasing the time given to the foundation subjects so that English and mathematics can receive more attention. This brings us to the question of how to safeguard the teaching of history at Key Stage 2.

The teaching and learning of history at Key Stage 2 would be safeguarded if a way could be found to teach it simultaneously with English. Indeed, this is a current requirement (QCA 1998: 5). The rest of this chapter looks at how reading skills and history skills can complement and enhance each other if taught in ways that acknowledge their own integrity and mutuality. First of all, does the act of being a reader and an historian have anything in common? It all depends on one's point of view. For the writers of this chapter, there are significant and exploitable points of similarity between the two activities which may be turned by the teacher into learning objectives.

Reading is, at heart, an active process which involves the ability to under-stand the thoughts and feelings of another mind via the medium of text (Pumfrey 1994). History, too, demands active involvement on the part of would-be historians. History is an investigative subject, a subject of enquiry and argument. Most of all, history is opinion. It is the job of the historian to try to establish fact in the secure knowledge that someone, somewhere will disagree. History is, indeed, argument without end. Partly because of the incompleteness of our picture of the past, we can all argue about the relative importance, reliability and partiality of the evidence. What needs to be taught within the subject of history is a questioning approach, where nothing is taken for granted.

There are obvious overlaps between what the reader does when approaching text and what the historian does when approaching primary and secondary written source material. History as process involves us in examination of sources and interpretations in a critical, appraising way to generate theories about their validity and reliability: historical methodology is characterised by scrupulous respect for evidence and disciplined use of the imagination.

Reading as process calls on the same schema. When reading, the reader engages in similar activities to the historian. The reader measures the writer's arguments, notes discrepancies in view points, observes plot development and critically analyses the character portrayals. Finally, there is the building up of justifiable opinions – about a person in the past (history) or about the quality of the formation of a central character (English). Having established that reading and history have common elements, it is necessary to devise teaching strategies which will systematically and sequentially develop the growing reader and historian simultaneously, where possible.

The two specific areas of the extension and development of reading on which we shall concentrate are all aspects of attention to text (word, sentence, paragraph levels) and information retrieval strategies. These are mutually supporting and essential for the reader:

> Only a minority of schools catered effectively for the teaching of advanced reading skills, particularly those related to information handling . . . in many of the schools the skills of seeking, scanning, selecting, comparing and evaluating information were given too little attention in most Key Stage 2 classes, and particularly at year 6.
>
> (DES 1991: 8)

We shall use history as the vehicle for ways to develop these with ideas for the History Study Unit on Victorian Britain. Ultimately, the activities suggested below should help improve the quality of teaching and learning in reading comprehension as well as aid the development of a range of reading strategies which the reader can use selectively and at will.

Planning the Victorian Britain History Study Unit

The approach we advocate for teaching history concentrates on the children finding out and their being taught to question what is taken for granted. This necessarily utilises primary source material and encourages the building of justifiable opinions by children. A glance at the history Key Elements will show that a questioning approach, adopted throughout the school, would almost certainly cover the range and depth of historical knowledge and understanding, interpretations of history and historical enquiry.

Importantly, teachers would be preparing their children for life in a society which increasingly presents opinions as facts, and half-truths as Gospel. A word of warning here about the sole use of textbooks and schemes of work to teach history: the teacher could end up concentrating less on actual historical investigation and argument and more on English comprehension exercises if care is not taken in their judicious use. The history taught the textbook way is only as good as the textbook. If the authors of the textbook

118

offer opinion as fact, provide poor historical background, and offer little chance for children to become skilled in the art of history, then the history being taught will not be particularly inspiring or fit the spirit of the Key Elements.

It is not good enough to plough through a textbook, ignoring the fundamental nature of history: that of investigating, enquiry and questioning. Without these aspects, and without reference to children acquiring the skills of historians, schools are indeed teaching English where they should be teaching history. These two subjects can be taught effectively and simultaneously in a history topic if the Key Elements are used as the foundation for teacher planning, as the following illustrative material indicates.

Skill: chronology

Placing events and people within a chronological framework is a fundamental historical skill. It is one way of making sense of text for the reader. A sequence of activities which can be adapted to suit individual needs with regard to ordering pictorial and written materials follows.

For the initial reader, pictures provide that all-important first step to understanding. Before print is on the page, activities which involve sequencing stories using pictures will begin to make the reader aware of language structure. Once the reader has grasped this, observation of historical objects allows numerous opportunities to link the printed word to the picture. Exercises could involve matching labels to objects (with or without word clues, for example, giving the initial letter of the word), or the activity could be extended to require the categorisation of objects into past and contemporary eras.

Matching sentences to photographs, where the reader goes beyond looking at a single object but must look at what is taking place in the picture, that is, the actions of the people – though still using picture cues, takes the connection between the visual text and the written word one stage further. Again, the use of sequencing is an important developmental aspect, and will assist the reader's ability to recognise organisation of text in the next stage of reading development where there are no picture cues. One suggested activity is to match sentences to the pictures, then put them in order on a timeline. For work on Victorian Britain, you could select pictures which would match captions such as the following:

- The world's first underground railway is built in London.
- The penny post is introduced.
- Victoria is crowned Queen.
- The first petrol-driven car is built by Karl Benz.
- Edison makes the first light bulb.

Skill: range and depth of historical understanding

Here the teacher must make a judgement about what the characteristic features of the Victorian Age were and how to make these relevant and available to her children as nascent historians. One area that immediately springs to mind is schooling now and then; another is the dwellings that people lived in then compared to today. It is the second part of this Key Element, the skill of describing and identifying reasons for and results of historical events, that might be more difficult to cover. It is essential to do because it is fundamental to the development of historical and reading skills. It is important to use both primary and secondary source material here to develop the reader and historian.

Looking at material to develop understanding of cause and effect – why events happened, and why people did things as they did – will also advance the literal reader into an inferential one. Questions of key importance in history of how, where, why, what and who can be used to help the reader infer information; again, the linkage of picture cues/diagrams with written text is helpful. (At a later stage in a reader's development, the comparison of historical sources acts in a similar way.) Traditional stories, myths, legends, biographies and autobiographies allow the exploration of development of understanding of plot, characters and language.

Awareness of what is fact and what is opinion through looking at different historical sources will also develop a reader's understanding of meaning; and once again, when looking at plot, activities which involve sequencing are relevant here. The passage below, an extract taken from *Mary Seacole*, by Sylvia Collicott, shows how a text about an historical figure can be used to help the reader deduce the difference between fact and opinion.

Reading skills

Read the passage below and then answer the questions which follow:

When Mary was a girl she watched her mother tend the sick in their hotel in Jamaica. Mary learnt how to look after sick people too. She learnt how to bring down a temperature and to mix medicine. Mary wanted to be a nurse. When she grew up she invented a remedy to cure people of a terrible sickness called cholera, which raged throughout Jamaica. She sailed to other countries called Panama and Cuba and set up hotels for the sick. But a war in Europe was to change Mary's life.

Russia invaded part of Turkey. Other countries joined in the fighting, including Britain. Mary's father had been a British soldier. He had told her stories of the horrors of war. She knew there would be many people who would need her help. So Mary decided to sail to England and ask the army officers if she could go and help the soldiers. In the days of Queen Victoria, women were not expected to go to war. When Mary arrived at the War Office in London, her offer of help was rudely turned down.

'Go away!' said the officers. 'We don't need your help.' But Mary was strong-minded and full of energy. She put on her blue bonnet with red ribbons and bought a ticket on a ship to Turkey.

(Collicott 1991: 98)

State whether these sentences are facts or opinions:

- When Mary was young, she lived in a hotel in Kingston, Jamaica.
- Mary liked looking after sick people.
- Mary invented a remedy to cure cholera.
- Mary sailed to England because she wanted to get permission to go out to the war.
- All officers do not like nurses.

Another exercise is to use the material to look at *plot* and character. For example, pupils could be asked to describe Mary Seacole's character, using events from the story to support their view; or they could be asked to complete a series of sentences appropriately, for example:

When Mary was young she:

- was sick in their hotel in Jamaica;
- watched her mother tend the sick in their hotel in Jamaica;
- did not like sick people.

OR

When Mary was young she   to other countries.
Mary wanted to be   watched her mother tend the sick.
Mary sailed   a nurse.

This type of sentence matching also teaches the pupil to observe punctuation.

Skill: interpretations of history

This is perhaps the most difficult of the Key Elements, and requires some conflict of source material. The study of history inevitably involves the examination of a variety of sources; through this, the historian takes a step beyond the literal – asking questions about when something was written and who wrote it – to asking questions about why it was written and what was its effect. Similarities and differences between sources, the past and present are made. Historical enquiry, identification of different viewpoints and interpretations of history progressively encourage the literal reader to take on a more inferential and certainly a more critical stance. Through comprehension, the reader is encouraged to think about the writer's viewpoints, bias and the use of language.

Source A: The Great Exhibition

On 1 May, 1851, Queen Victoria opened the Great Exhibition in the Crystal Palace, Hyde Park, London. The Exhibition building was designed by Joseph Paxton and made entirely of iron and glass. The iron framework was lifted into place a section at a time by two huge iron cranes. The Exhibition was the idea of Prince Albert. It was very successful with over 100,000 different exhibits including those loaned by the Queen herself. Models of all types, agricultural tools, household equipment, clocks, furniture, and scientific instruments were on show. Admission to the public cost one shilling from Mondays to Thursdays and half-a-crown on Fridays and Saturdays (1s and 2/6d). The Exhibition lasted for five months and over six million people visited it, many coming by trains.

There was no doubt that the Exhibition was an outstanding success. Built in less than seven months, it showed British achievements in all their glory and emphasised that this country was the 'workshop of the world' . . .

After the Exhibition, the Crystal Palace building was dismantled and rebuilt in South London. Unfortunately, it was destroyed by fire in November, 1936.

(Perkins and Perkins 1995: 42)

Source B: What is the Crystal Palace?

From a special correspondent:

This is the most interesting question of the day. It is a great system of education – the education of the eye – the education of facts. Such is the Crystal Palace Institution. Its material, construction, and internal arrangements, are one huge lesson in physical science – a lesson on objects to engineers, mechanics, artists, and all sorts of craftsmen in glass, wood and metal.

A visit to the Palace is, therefore, a duty which man owes to himself . . . And a visit to it is not a duty to be hurried over like a lesson repeated by rote . . .

(Extract from the *Manchester Examiner and Times*, 3 June 1854)

Questions

1 To what event does source A refer?
2 Are sources A and B primary or secondary sources? How do you know this?
3 Name three types of exhibits you might find at the Exhibition.
4 What does the author of source B mean when he describes the Crystal Palace Institution as 'the education of the eye' (line 2)?
5 Why does the author of source A refer to Britain as 'the workshop of the world'?
6 Why do you think the Great Exhibition was successful? Give reasons for your answer.
7 What did the author of source B mean when he said the Exhibition was 'not a duty to be hurried over like a lesson repeated by rote' (lines 9–10)?
8 Do you think the author of source B enjoyed his visit to the Crystal Palace? Give reasons for your answer.

Skill: historical enquiry

Focusing historical enquiry on a particular Study Unit, such as Victorian Britain, enables the teacher to plan for the development of reading comprehension and a range of reading strategies through this topic. All the previous ideas for skill development so far described have been 'free standing' as it were. It is necessary that they are embedded within classroom topic work and not used as isolated skill development exercises. This view grows out of research findings. Searching for and reporting on information found in written materials is something children find very difficult to do and they need guided practice in information retrieval skills (DES 1975; Neville and Pugh 1975, 1977; Maxwell 1977; Lunzer and Gardner 1979; Southgate *et al.* 1981; Wray 1985; Wray and Lewis 1992).

Evidence points to a gap between children's verbal knowledge of information strategies and their actual use. When children did find information in books or written materials, the most common strategy for making a record of it was to write it down. How can this state of affairs be tackled in the busy classroom? Wray and Lewis (1992: 22) are unequivocal: 'Children needed guided practice in using the system and the books, as well as explanations of how to do so.'

Lunzer and Gardner (1979) recommended that situations be devised which foster a willingness (on the part of the children) to reflect on what is read. This is not helped by the indiscriminate use of exercises in English or history textbooks where the reader is not expected to bring much previous knowledge to the text. If the texts are set out as isolated passages without any introduction or thematic links then they will not assist in building schematic bridges between the reader's previous knowledge and the text. Beard (1994: 142) makes the point forcibly: the traditional layout of exercises dictates the fact that questions have to be used to test comprehension rather than facilitate it.

Teachers will benefit from close observation of children's behaviour when involved in locating information in written materials. They can tailor their teaching according to the levels of skills the children display. They will need to ensure that children possess (or are in the process of possessing) the skills necessary to undertake project work efficiently. The suitability in terms of content, language structures used and readability level of the resources must be matched to the children's attainments and interests. Ultimately, the teacher will be fostering the research skills of the historian and reader. This will be easier if both teacher and children approach the topic purposefully.

One approach is to highlight the project's purpose as the answering of questions posed by the children themselves. Because history is presented in a variety of ways and is embedded in all subjects, the 'topic' approach will inevitably generate questions in a number of areas. A shared class story about life in a cotton factory or a newspaper account about someone's journey on a railway for the first time may provoke enquiry about how mills work, whether they are still in use today, why the railways were invented or what type of transport was in use previously.

Such historical questions posed by the children offer unlimited opportunity for them to develop information retrieval and research skills. The questions will also indicate the source material that needs to be collected and the information texts to be accessed; historical questions about the British Empire and Commonwealth may warrant use of the index pages in an atlas as well as an historical text. Examination of an object visually may stimulate enquiry as to how something works, its function and purpose, necessitating use of science and technological texts. These questions will provide a framework for discussing the steps that children would follow throughout the topic. The overall structure and direction of the topic is then driven significantly (though not completely) by the children's desire to find out. This motivation will help sustain the search for information and the creation of the finished product.

In conclusion, vital to the overall progression in reading is the development of reading skills; in particular the understanding of how a text is organised; the ability to use a contents/index page and a glossary; and understanding of character and formation of plot. The study of history not only offers ample opportunity for the promotion of all these skills but actively encourages it.

Research of historical information, people and events necessitates the pupil historian knowing how to obtain information. Reference books, information books and encyclopaedias present a rich collection for the teacher to devise suitable questions about the contents and index pages, as shown in this example:

Contents

Questions on the contents page

1   On what page would you find out about Victorian clothes?
2   On what page would you find the introduction?
3   What would you find out about on page 8?
4   What would you find out about on page 10?
5   What would you find out about on page 20?
6   When did Queen Victoria begin her reign?
7   On what page would you find out about the telephone?
8   On what page would you find out about entertainment in Victorian London?

Dictionary exercises are also useful here, for example, looking up vocabulary to answer questions about the period, and comparing/contrasting it with its use today:

Victorian Dictionary Quiz

Look up these words using a dictionary, then match to the sentence below:

census, back to back, coronation, governess, monitor, slum, textiles, tram, penny farthing, nanny

1 Official record of the number of people in a population.

2 Describes two rows of houses with their backs closely facing each other.

3 Woman employed to look after children in a nursery.

4 Type of bus powered by electricity and running on rails.

5 Bicycle with a big wheel in front and a small one behind.

6 Ceremony of crowning a monarch.

7 Goods made from woollen cloth.

8 Woman employed to teach and train children in a family.

9 Area of crowded squalid houses.

10 Child who taught simple lessons to younger ones.

(Adapted from Perkins and Perkins 1995: 78)

Cloze procedure

Development of historical understanding is actively assisted through knowledge of historical language. Cloze procedure involves the deletion of selected or random words in a text, leaving spaces in which the pupil substitutes appropriate vocabulary. This technique, using historical sources or vocabulary connected with a period, will help to produce more effective readers.

When using cloze procedure with younger children, it is helpful to use historical reading material that includes repetition, such as nursery rhymes, poems and songs. Material of this kind is useful not only because it allows pupils to identify different ways in which the past is represented, but also because, for the early reader, rhyming material links phonics to the learning process.

It is also useful for the pupil unused to cloze procedure to begin by underlining words in a passage which they regard as being the most important. With history, exercises may be based on historical understanding and vocabulary associated with a topic or an aspect of a topic that the reader will come across frequently. For example, in a passage about Victorian transport, pupils could be asked to underline words connected with rail transportation. For the more advanced reader, these exercises could then involve filling in the correct noun or adjective, for example, as in the passage below:

Read through the following passage, and then fill in the missing words from the list at the end.

Victorian clothes

Like today, how much Victorians spent on clothes depended on how much money they possessed. Unlike _____, though, Victorian dress was very different from modern day fashions.

In _____ times, working class clothes were usually made of wool. _____ wore trousers and shirts, and girls a dress with a _____. Poor children often went without shoes, because they were too _____.

Families who were wealthy wore silk or sometimes velvet. Men wore _____ coats over their trousers and shirts, and often carried a cane and _____.

Wealthy women wore wide skirts held out by _____ and very tightly laced corsets. Bonnets were also very _____.

frock boys expensive pinafore Victorian crinolines today popular gloves

---

Skill: organisation and communication

The final act of the historian who has defined research questions about some aspect of the past, and located and selected information to answer them, is to organise his or her thoughts and opinions about the findings and communicate them to an audience. This will necessitate being able to sift through material, comprehend it, evaluate it and finally summarise it, including one's judgements and opinions with it.

Eden (1991) was concerned that her pupils were at times not able to grasp the meaning of texts and found they lacked the knowledge of the structure and register of some information texts. She claims that using the ERICA (Effective Reading in Content Areas) model has helped her children acquire such knowledge. This model identified four stages in the study process which had to be explicated and modelled for the children:

1   preparing for reading: to give a logical framework for information from the text;
2   thinking through the reading: to provide opportunities for pupils to interact with the text;
3   extracting and organising information to summarise the text in their own words;
4   translating information to clarify and internalise concepts through writing.

This four-stage process may usefully be borne in mind by teachers when planning for information retrieval work in history.

Conclusion

The acquisition of historical skills and reading skills past the initial stages of learning to read can be facilitated by planning History Study Units with reference to the Key Elements and through activities that are related to these skills. This method presents children with the opportunities to be historians, to discover information for themselves and to work out how to use it, skills necessary not just for history, but for life as well.

References

Beard, R. (1994) *Developmental Reading 3–13*, Sevenoaks, Kent: Hodder and Stoughton.

Bright, M. (1997) 'Strict New School Day for All Primary Children', *Observer*, 8 June.

Carvel, J. (1997a) 'Blunkett Aims for Basic Three R's in Primary Schools', *Guardian*, 14 May.

Carvel, J. (1997b) 'Start Foreign Languages at 7', *Guardian*, 29 May.

Collicott, S. (1991) 'Mary Seacole' in Ginn History, Key Stage One: Teachers Resource Book, Aylesbury Bucks: Ginn.

Department for Education and Employment (DfEE) (1997) *Results of 1996 National Curriculum Assessments of 11-year-olds in England*, London: DfEE.

Department of Education and Science (DES) (1975) *A Language for Life* (Bullock Report), London: HMSO.

—— (1991) *The Teaching and Learning of Reading in Primary Schools*, London: HMSO.

Eden, J.E. (1991) 'Teaching Pupils to Read for Information', *Reading*, 25: 8–12.

Lawrie, J. and Noble, P. (1990) *Victorian Times*, London: Unwin Hyman.

Lunzer, E. and Gardner, K. (1979) *The Effective Use of Reading*, London: Heinemann.

Maxwell, J. (1977) *Reading Progress from 8–15*, Windsor, Berks: National Foundation for Educational Research.

Neville, M. and Pugh, A. (1975) 'Reading Ability and Ability to Use a Book', *Reading*, 9, 3: 23–31.

Neville, M. and Pugh, A. (1977) 'Ability to Use a Book: Further Studies', *Reading*, 11, 3: 13–22.

Office for Standards in Education (OFSTED) (1997) *The Annual Report of Her Majesty's Chief Inspector of Schools*, London: HMSO.

Perkins, D.C. and Perkins, E.J. (1995) *Victorian Britain: Master File Key Stages 2–3*, Swansea: Domino Books.

Pumfrey, P. (1994) *Children's Difficulties in Reading, Spelling and Writing*, Lewes, Sussex: Falmer Press.

Qualifications and Curriculum Authority (QCA) (1998) *Maintaining breadth and balance at Key Stages 1 and 2*, Hayes, Middlesex: QCA Publication.

Southgate, V., Arnold, H. and Johnson, S. (1981) *Extending Beginning Reading*, London: Heinemann.

Wray, D. (1985) *Teaching Information Skills Through Project Work*, Sevenoaks, Kent: Hodder and Stoughton.

Wray, D. and Lewis, M. (1992) 'Primary Children's Use of Information Books', *Reading*, 26, 3: 19–24.

9

LIFE IN TUDOR TIMES
The use of written sources

Joan Blyth

Throughout the 1995 History National Curriculum for Key Stages 1 and 2, emphasis is put on the use and interpretation of original source material. Key Element 4 on 'historical enquiry' refers to 'a range of sources of information, including documents and printed sources' (DfE 1995: 5). The level descriptions, particularly for level 5, also refer to children 'beginning to evaluate sources of information'. So far, little has been published to help teachers find suitable, reasonably short extracts from sources relating to personalities and social history. There are rather more for political, military and parliamentary events. This is particularly true for Key Stage 1 and for Study Units 1 and 2 for Key Stage 2. The 1995 omission of the Stuarts should enable more time to be spent on the concentrated study of a particular contemporary Tudor source.

The chief concern of this book is the interdependence of English and history. The English attainment targets of listening and speaking, reading and writing are essential skills to enable children to further the historical Key Elements of knowledge and understanding, interpretation, enquiry and communication. To make use of a written source in history children must be able to read and understand that source as well as to listen to the teacher explaining it. Further to this, handwriting and the meaning of words are additional skills needed to use language in historical sources, especially those before the nineteenth century. Thus sources used for History Study Units 1 and 2 require these additional skills.

A further link between English and history, apart from the language of sources, is the actual content of the History Study Units. In the case of 'Life in Tudor times', Shakespeare is listed as part of 'ways of life of people at different levels of society', with examples of the Elizabethan theatre (DfE 1995: 7). Many primary schools are introducing work on this topic through drama, especially in view of the interest in the newly constructed Globe Theatre in London. Information about Shakespeare for teachers and primary pupils is now more readily available. For example, Dorothy Turner's *William*

Shakespeare (1985) is a short biography with full-colour illustrations, a list of 'new words' (for example, 'forebidding' (p. 5) and a bibliography. She recommends the Ladybird book *William Shakespeare* (1981) for children to read. A more recent book is Bradbury's *Shakespeare and his Theatre* (1990) which also has a glossary of Elizabethan words, closely linked to language work. An even more recent book on similar lines is Jane Shuter's *Shakespeare and the Theatre* (1996). Queen Elizabeth I was herself interested in plays, and a rare contemporary source describes her enjoyment of *Palamon and Arcite* at Christ Church, Oxford, in 1565 (Blyth and Hughes 1997: 43–4). Primary schools are increasingly dramatising appropriate Shakespeare plays with simplified text.

With the many changes in the primary curriculum during the past seven years, most teachers have been too busy to read enough to teach any part of a Study Unit in depth. Therefore they have been unable to use sources of any length and have concentrated on 'speech bubbles' in the double page spread of the new textbooks for children to read, such as Queen Elizabeth's speech before the Armada (Blyth 1992: 11). At most stages of the primary school, contemporary pictures are a great help in understanding a text or a source. These are difficult to find in relation to a particular source, and care should be taken to locate contemporary pictures instead of artists' impressions or sketches from textbooks. Reading pictures and the writing on them is yet another skill linking history with English (see Chapter 5)

A final problem for teachers is to bring out how the detailed incident related in the source fits into the whole Study Unit. This is an issue in any primary history teaching, depending as it does in part on the capacity of young children to conceptualise society in any period of time. This and the other general issues already mentioned can be illustrated from an actual example:

An Elizabethan Fagin

Some of the rogues inhabiting the Elizabethan underworld came from well-to-do backgrounds. The one referred to below was taken into custody by William Fleetwood, the indefatigable Recorder of London. Fleetwood's description of him, contained in a letter to Burghley, is reminiscent of Charles Dickens' Fagin.

Amongst our travels this one matter tumbled out of the way, that one Wotton, a gentleman-born and sometime merchant-man of good credit, who falling by time into decay kept an ale-house at Smart's Quay near Billingsgate, and after that, for some misdemeanour being put down, he reared up a new kind of life, and in the same house he procured all the cutpurses about this city to repair to his said house. There was a school-house set up to learn young boys to cut purses. There were hung up two devices; the one was a pocket, the other a purse. The pocket had in it certain counters and was hung about with hawks' bells and over the top did hang a little sacring-bell; and he that could take out a counter without any noise was allowed to be a public foister; and he that could take a piece of silver out of the purse without the noise of any of the bells, he was adjudged a judicial nipper . . . Nota that a foister is a pickpocket and a nipper is termed a pickpurse or cutpurse.

(Tawney and Power [1924] 1951, ii: 337–9)

The source used by children in this chapter relates to poor boys trained as pickpockets by a once prosperous 'gentleman-born and sometime a merchant-man of good credit'. This should be used as part of 'ways of life of people at different levels of society' (DfE 1995: 7) for the City of London in the late sixteenth century. It illustrates one part of the 'ways of life in town and country' already suggested as a component of 'Life in Tudor Times', namely the condition of the urban poor. In this instance the relation of the rich to the poor is shown to be more complicated than textbooks sometimes suggest.

A version of the source itself in modern English is given later (p. 138), for teachers will need to master it before children can be led to understand the meaning of this source. They will then be in a position to explain the sixteenth-century language, to discuss it with the class (putting up the new words for the children to see) and then use the transcription to enable the children to use the source and to make inferences from it. For example, the first sentence of this source reads in the original: 'Amongst our travels this one matter tumbled out of the way', which can be transcribed thus into modern English: 'I happened to come across this case when on my travels.' William Fleetwood was a magistrate, and travelled round London more than most people did.

Any extract such as this also allows for developing other ways, most of them already mentioned, in which the needs and claims of English and history coincide in the primary curriculum: enquiry and interpretation, weighing of evidence, listening, reading and writing, imaginative reconstruction and moral judgement. Table 9.1 summarises the extent to which this source can help to fulfil the requirements of the National Curriculum.

Perhaps a small year 6 class with unusually capable children, in an area where a high level of literacy is normal, could use this source with spectacular

Table 9.1 Interrelation of history and English in the National Curriculum, using 'An Elizabethan Fagin'

History Key Elements	English Attainment Targets
Chronology (a little) Knowledge and understanding	Speaking and listening: 're-present important features [of material]' (Key Skill 2b)
Interpretation	" " "
Historical enquiry (none)	Reading: range 'texts drawn from a variety of cultures and traditions' (1d)
Organisation and communication	're-present information in different forms' (Key Skill 2c)
Recommended emphases in Study Unit 2	
ways of life of people at different levels of society: town and country	Writing: 'opportunities to plan, draft and improve their work on paper and on screen' (2b); 'use punctuation marks correctly' (2c)

results. What follows shows what can be achieved by an experienced teacher with a year 5 class in what would, by any criterion, be recognised as an average school in an urban area.

Case study 1: 'An Elizabethan Fagin' with year 5

Jean Matthews is an established teacher at St Hilda's Church of England Aided Primary School in Stretford, Greater Manchester. She offered to teach her class of thirty-two children aged 9–10 (year 5) with an average spread of ability according to the school's customary Richmond test, using this particular source. The school in which she works is at present a single-stream school with about 260 children in the infant and junior phases. She spends twenty weeks with one hour in each week on history and in this time covers the Tudor unit. Her resources hitherto have consisted of basic textbooks from Heinemann, though not the support book from the same publisher: *The Poor in Tudor England* by Jane Shuter (1996). There are single copies of some lightweight Tudor reference books and reference material in the library, as well as resource boxes to hand. She also keeps in reserve a set of 'Unsteads'[1] on the Tudors and Stuarts – carefully preserved in a cupboard in case of need, which did not arise on this occasion. When they first encountered 'An Elizabethan Fagin', her class had come to the end of selected work on other aspects of life in Tudor times, including the collective production of an impressive wall frieze on the Armada. I then helped the teacher with the preparation of her two sessions on 'An Elizabethan Fagin': two hours was all the time that could be spared for this purpose.

The teacher chose this extract from three possible sources relating to Tudor times. The other two sources, reproduced below, were a contemporary description of a rogue, by Thomas Dekker, in 1567, and a list of a poor man's property as shown in a probate inventory of 1599. All three had been selected by John Pound for his *Poverty and Vagrancy in Tudor England* (1977). The language problem would actually have been less acute in the other two sources but she felt that the content would have been less stimulating for this particular class. All three sources are transcribed from the original handwritten ones.

A contemporary description of a rogue

Harman, in his 'Caveat for Common Cursetors', published in 1567, lists no fewer than twenty-four different types of vagrant. The men and women referred to in the following documents are typical of many of their class.

A rogue is known to all men by his name, but not all men by his conditions; no puritan can dissemble more than he, for he will speak in a lamentable tune and crawl along the streets, (supporting his body by a staff) as if there were not life enough in him to put strength into his legs: his head shall be bound about with linen, loathsome to behold; and as filthy in colour as the complexion of his face; his apparel is all tattered, his bosom naked, and most commonly no shirt on: not that they are driven to this misery by mere want, but that if they had better clothes given them, they would rather sell them to some of their own fraternity than wear them, and wander up and down in that piteous manner, only to move people to compassion, and to be relieved with money, which being gotten, at night is spent as merrily and as lewdly as in the day it was won by counterfeit villany. Another sect there be of these, and they are called STURDY ROGUES: these walk from county to county under colour of travelling to their friends or to find out some kinsman, or else to deliver a letter to one gentleman or other, whose name he will have fairly endorsed on paper folded up for that purpose, and handsomely sealed: others use this shift to carry a Certificate or passport about them, with the hand or seal of some Justice to it, . . . all these writings are but counterfeit, they having amongst them (of their own RANK), that can write and read, who are their secretaries in this business.

(Thomas Dekker, *Bell-Man of London: A Discovery of all the idle Vagabonds in England: their conditions: their laws amongst themselves: their degrees and orders: their meetings, and their manners of living, (both men and women)*, London, 1608, quoted by P.J. Helm, *England under the Yorkists and Tudors, 1471–1603*, London: Bell, 1968; and in Pound 1977: 98)

A poor man's property

The following inventory gives an impression of a poor man's possessions at the end of the sixteenth century. The labourer concerned was more fortunate than most, for he did at least have some property to leave.

A true and perfect inventorye of all and singuler the goods and chattells of Thomas Herries late deceased in the parishe of St. Gregoryes in Norwich prysed by us William Rogers and Gregorye Wesbye the xv[th] daye of October in the yeare of our Lord God 1599

In primis:	one borded bedsted	3s. 4d.
Item:	one mattresse and one under cloathe	1s. 6d.
Item:	one flocke bed	2s. 6d.
Item:	one bolster	2s. 0d.
Item:	one downe pillowe and an old cushaigne	1s. 6d.
Item:	two leather pillowes filled with feathers	3s. 4d.
Item:	one payer of shetes	2s. 0d.
Item:	one bed blanket	1s. 8d.
Item:	one old cofer	2s. 0d.
Item:	one drye barrell	3d.
Item:	2 salt boxes	1s. 0d.
Item:	one hake, a fryer pann, a payer of tonges and a rostinge yron	1s. 6d.
Item:	one litle ketle, a sawer and 3 pewter spoones	2s. 6d.
Item:	3 little boles	1s. 0d.
Item:	one ketle, one potspone, 28 trenyens	1s. 0d.
Item:	2 woodinge platters and 5 dishes and twoo erthen potts	8d.
Item:	a stone pott and 5 galley pottes	4d.
Item:	a hamper and certen old washe	6d.
Item:	4 frayles and 2 stooles	6d.
Item:	a little table and 4 stoles	3s. 0d.
Item:	3 chiselles, 2 hamers and a perser	8d.

Item:	3 old cushings	6d.
Item:	2 payers of hand cuffes and one dozen of hand kerchers and an old pillowbere	2s. 6d.
Item:	2 old shirtes	1s. 8d.
Item:	one old forme and 2 old cappes	1s. 0d.
Total:		£1 18s. 5d.

[The sums of money were given in Roman numerals in the original inventory.]

(Quoted in Pound 1962: 121)

In the first of the two sessions, 'An Elizabethan Fagin' was introduced at considerable length through lively oral work. First, the teacher talked about the children going shopping today; about how easy it is to steal from unaware shoppers; and about how important it is to secure your money when shopping. To show that poverty and unemployment were widespread in Tudor England as well as nowadays, she referred to the TV play *The Prince and the Pauper*, which some of the class had watched. She then turned to the source and discussed the meaning of 'Elizabethan' and also the reference in the title and preamble to Dickens's *Oliver Twist*, which some of the children knew. Each pair of children was provided with an enlarged copy of the source, and also with a double page spread of pictures: of pockets and purses hanging from gentlemen's belts; a Tudor street scene; and a rich gentleman in Tudor costume; these had been copied from various other sources which she had available. Importantly, she emphasised that the existence of our source showed that this was something which had actually happened, for it was part of a letter sent by William Fleetwood to Lord Burghley, Queen Elizabeth's chief minister, about Mr Wotton, whom he had imprisoned for training boys to be pickpockets.

Then the children read the source document silently. Further discussion with the teacher subsequently showed that although they could read it, many could not understand the meaning owing to the Elizabethan words and syntax. More frequent use of Tudor sources or the provision of support in reading the document would help to overcome this.

Five tasks were written on the board and each child chose one of these to start in the first session and continue in the other, which took place on the following day. The tasks were:

• Imagine you are a young boy in Elizabethan times and explain how you were taught to steal. How did you feel about it?
• Write all you know about Mr Wotton. Was he an honest man? How can you guess?

- How did Mr Wotton teach the boys to become pickpockets?
- Rewrite the passage in modern English.
- Draw an Elizabethan gentleman and make sure you show his purse and pocket. Where will the purse and pocket be on this costume?

The children started work after discussion of the tasks and completed this work in the second session.

Nine of the children chose to write about the imaginative task: this produced the best results. They were neatly written, though one child started each new sentence on a new line so the outcome appeared disjointed. All the others wrote in one large paragraph (see Figure 9.1). Although punctuation and spelling are not perfect in the figure, the imaginative involvement is obvious. It brings out the way in which homeless and hungry boys were trapped into living with Mr Wotton and taught to be pickpockets and cutpurses.

The second example (Figure 9.2) refers to London, Billingsgate, Queen Elizabeth I, Charles Dickens and St Paul's Cathedral, and brings out the difference between pickpockets (foisters) and cutpurses (nippers), words

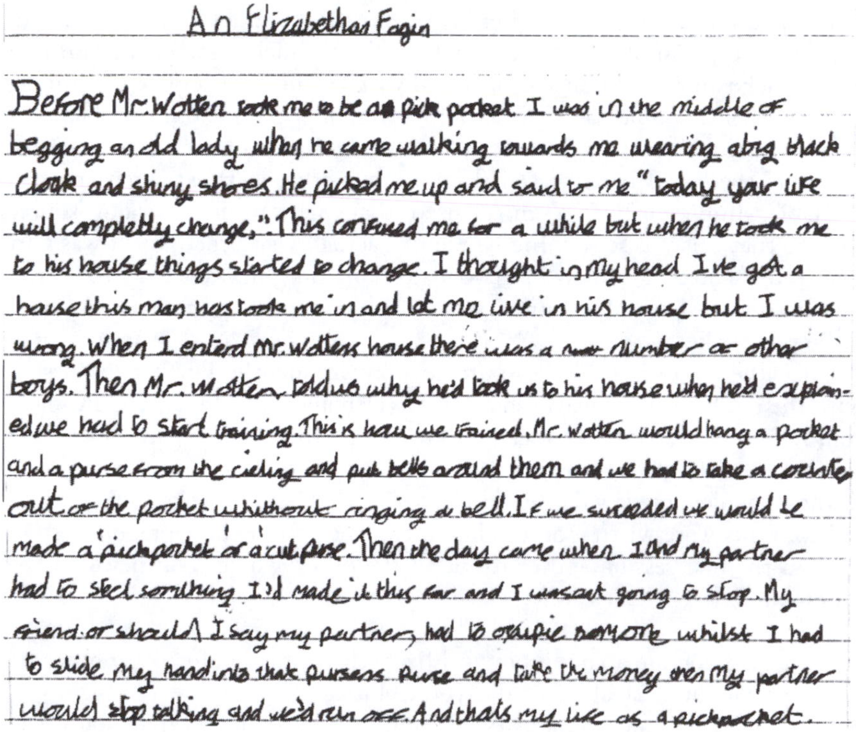

An Elizabethan Fagin

Before Mr. Wotten took me to be an pick pocket I was in the middle of begging an old lady when he came walking towards me wearing a big black cloak and shiny shoes. He picked me up and said to me "today your life will completly change." This confused me for a while but when he took me to his house things started to change. I thought in my head I've got a house this man has took me in and let me live in his house but I was wrong. When I enterd Mr. Wottens house there was a new number of other boys. Then Mr. Wotten told us why he'd took us to his house when he'll explained we had to start training. This is how we trained. Mr. Wotten would hang a pocket and a purse from the cieling and put bells around them and we had to take a coinite out of the pocket whithout ringing a bell. If we suceeded we would be made a pickpocket or a cutpurse. Then the day came when I and my partner had to steal something I'd made it this far and I wasn't going to stop. My friend or should I say my partner had to occupie someone whilst I had to slide my hand into that pursess purse and take the money then my partner would stop talking and we'd run off. And thats my life as a pickpocket.

Figure 9.1 Work of a nine-year-old on 'An Elizabethan Fagin' – I

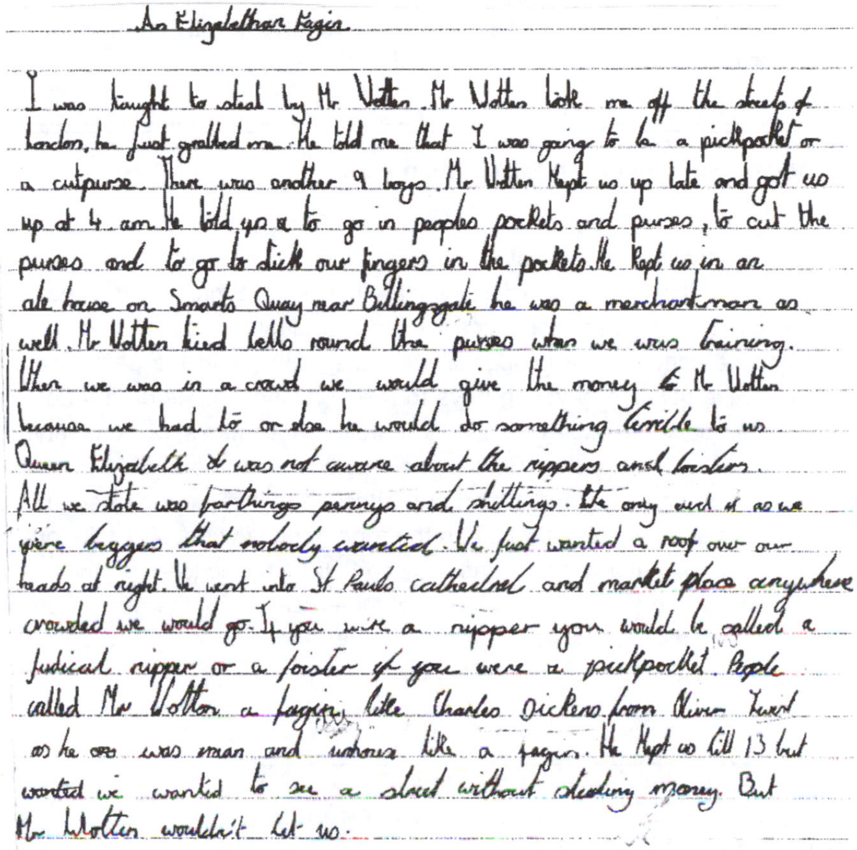

An Elizabethan Fagin

I was taught to steal by Mr Wotton. Mr Wotton took me off the streets of London, he just grabbed me. He told me that I was going to be a pickpocket or a cutpurse. There was another 9 boys. Mr Wotton kept us up late and got us up at 4 am. He told us e to to go in peoples pockets and purses, to cut the purses and to go to stick our fingers in the pockets. He kept us in an ale house on Smarts Quay near Billingsgate he was a merchant man as well. Mr Wotton tied bells round the purses when we was training. When we was in a crowd we would give the money to Mr Wotton because we had to or else he would do something terrible to us. Queen Elizabeth I was not aware about the rippers and foisters. All we stole was farthings pennys and shillings. the only work of us we were beggers that nobody wanted. We just wanted a roof over our heads at night. We went into St Pauls cathedral and market place anywhere crowded we would go. If you were a nypper you would be called a judical nypper or a foister if you were a pickpocket. People called Mr Wotton a fagin, like Charles Dickens from Oliver Twist as he was was mean and unkind like a fagin. He kept us till 13 but wanted we wanted to see a street without stealing money. But Mr Wotton wouldn't let us.

Figure 9.2 Work of a nine-year-old on 'An Elizabethan Fagin' – II

which are of course still in use though with changed meanings. The idea that the Queen would inevitably disapprove of the dishonesty involved shows how much children still identify the monarchy with virtue. This girl's reference to Billingsgate located the source in a place famous still for its fish market as well as in Tudor times. She also saw the relevance of Oliver Twist, though it is not clear whether she had grasped the 'then/then' difference between Tudor and Victorian times as well as the 'then/now' difference between Tudor times and today, always a conceptual problem in primary history.

The task least well done was 'writing the passage in your own words'. Seven children attempted this. It was a difficult task for them. They summarised it rather than transcribing it in their own words. Their paragraphs were shorter than the original. Most children did not use the italicised introduction to help them. It was here that they could have found that William Fleetwood had sent this letter to Lord Burghley about Mr Wotton's imprisonment. The version in modern English which follows is almost the same length as the original:

Modern version of 'An Elizabethan Fagin'

I happened to come across this case when on my travels. Mr Wotton, born a gentleman and at one time a well-liked merchant, came upon bad times. He then kept an ale-house at Smart's Quay near Billingsgate. He was imprisoned because of some bad behaviour. When he came out of prison he started a new life in the same ale-house. He persuaded young boys to live in his house. Here he taught them to become expert at stealing from gentlemen's pockets and purses. He hung up two devices: one was a pocket, the other a purse. The pocket had counters in it and he attached to it some bells used by falconers and also an altar bell on the top. The boy who could take out a counter without any noise was allowed to be a public foister. The boy who could take a piece of silver out of the purse, or cut the purse from a gentleman's belt, without noise of any kind was called a skilled nipper . . . Note that a foister is a pickpocket and a nipper a pick-purse or cutpurse.

In general, the teacher's own appraisal of the lesson was that the class had performed well for an average year 5. They enjoyed doing this unusual in-depth work, asked many questions in the second session while completing their tasks and also talked about this kind of study. One parent was impressed by her child's knowledge of pickpockets in Tudor times and viewed the whole exercise favourably. All the children expressed the moral view that Mr Wotton was very wrong to train children to steal and said that they would not want to be trained for such a purpose. I would add that, even if they thought that this is what they were expected to say, they were in no doubt about that message.

The children found sixteenth-century language difficult, as expected, and the teacher felt pressurised by the time constraint so she could not elucidate it sufficiently. This time constraint was partly the outcome of various contingencies in arranging this joint project, for the Aztecs were looming before I could complete our plans. Perhaps if less time had been spent on introducing the source and more on the children's own reading and comprehension of it there might have been a little less pressure. The teacher agrees that in future she could use such source material at an earlier point, for example during her work on Tudor towns. Since she regularly uses present-day source material in language work, she now feels that it would be of great value to incorporate a source such as 'An Elizabethan Fagin' to link history with English. It could also be a stimulus to role-play and a way of initiating discussion on Elizabethan script, language and spelling.

My own assessment of the children's work was that the written outcome was very varied in relation to their small range of ability. The two extracts in Figures 9.1 and 9.2 were completed in an hour and a quarter by quite able children. At the other extreme, a few managed only five lines in the same time or just drew a small 'Elizabethan gentleman' without labels to name parts of the costume. Advice for another similar piece of work would be to give each child a full transcription of the source after discussion with them and before they started their individual tasks. They would then not have a transcription exercise among their choice of tasks, but could undertake the other assignments more confidently. After redrafting, the final piece of work could then be put into their history files as a momento of the topic and as possible material for future consultation or revision, for example by London children in a local history study or part of Tudor London, perhaps of Billingsgate.

Case study 2: 'An Elizabethan Fagin' with year 6

Pat Hoodless used the 'Elizabethan Fagin' source with a year 6 class at Didsbury Road Junior School, in Stockport. These are her comments:

I worked for about forty-five minutes with a mixed ability class of thirty children. The class had recently been working on 'Life in Tudor Times' and had just completed a field trip to London in connection with this theme. It was a difficult time to introduce such work, however, at the end of the term and as in the previous case study there was a sense of being rushed. The class teacher and myself talked to them, explaining that they could work in pairs, talk about the document, find out as much as they could about what was happening in it, and tell us their shared feelings after reading it. We allowed about twenty minutes for this activity. In the first instance the children used the document in its original form and were given no support in reading the text. After reading and discussing their findings, they read the modern version and made further comments.

Two main features characterised their responses. One was their level of confidence in handling the source. This varied considerably. Some moderately able children were totally at a loss and were so daunted that they made little effort to pursue the task. Some children of low reading ability, not realising the complexity of the task, made inspired guesses at what was happening, but showed little real understanding. A group of children with middle to high ability in reading attempted interpretations, but misunderstandings of key vocabulary confused them. Two children of high ability, however, coped well with the document, while one boy was able to understand and communicate the gist of it quite accurately. He was used to reading old-fashioned books, he told us, and had not found it particularly difficult. He had also understood the significance of the title and seemed a very literate child in the broadest sense of the word. Experience in handling different types of text appeared to have influenced this child's confidence and possibly also his ability in using the document.

The other significant feature of the children's responses was their interest level. This was generally high throughout the class, despite the reading difficulty of the text. The children were genuinely interested in the strange typeface, the spellings and the long words such as 'misdemeanour'. There is a clear opportunity in this kind of task to explore language in an archaic form, comparing it with modern usage. This is in itself a valuable aspect of literacy as well as involving the historical concept of continuity and change. While some were quite overwhelmed by the request to try to find out what they could from the source, their interest level was considerably raised when the modern version was given out and the meaning of the source was clarified. Possibly, their original failure to extract meaning motivated their interest in the subsequent explanation.

Conclusions about strategies in using material of this kind included the following:

- There is a need for considerable support for children in using such texts, in the form of alerting them to potential difficulties and providing explanations of difficult words or phrases.
- Children might work more successfully in mixed ability groups, to improve the quality of interaction and understanding.
- It might be advantageous to make earlier or simultaneous use of the modern version.

The overall conclusion was that better responses would have been achieved if we had carried out a significant amount of preparation and provided guidance and well focused discussion with the whole class before attempting a difficult activity like this with children of such varied ability. As a challenging task for the very able, confident readers, however, this was a very appropriate piece of historical text for them to work on independently.

Other kinds of written sources for Tudor times

The 'Fagin' source was a letter from the sixteenth century. There are other types of source suitable for primary classes to use when studying Tudor history (Fines and Nichol 1997: 81–97), for example probate inventories, lists of property and its value at the end of wills. In these documents the handwriting is very variable, especially in the case of inventories written not by professional scriveners but by friends or relatives who could only just write at all. For example, the inventory of Robert Brerewood of Chester in 1601 is in a very difficult hand with crossing out and insertions and doubtful words with which even a professional archivist might find some difficulty (Blyth and Hughes 1997: 87). Some informed and inspired guesses against a background of thorough knowledge of the period may be needed.

Other useful types of source for the Tudor period (Emmison 1967) include: parish registers, indicating family history, for some parishes from the later sixteenth century onwards (West 1982, 1983); contemporary topographical accounts, quite often printed (for example, the rows of Chester: see Blyth and Hughes 1997: 86); maps such as John Speed's county maps with town plan insets (Nicolson 1988); royal charters where relevant; and inscriptions on church monuments and brasses from the sixteenth century (among many other periods). Among these, too, handwritten sources are usually more difficult to read than those which were printed or professionally carved. By the middle of the sixteenth century printing presses, originally from the continent, began to be used for official records. Many local record offices now employ an archive education officer who can introduce classes of children, including primary children, to Tudor sources.

So there is considerable scope for teachers with initiative, such as Jean Matthews, to develop work with written sources, as the history National Curriculum suggests. It is to be hoped that as they become more at ease with the National Curriculum they will find time to use these sources and thereby benefit work in both history and English.

Note

1 R.J. Unstead, a primary school headmaster, wrote many historical texts for children from the 1950s until his quite recent death. Long before the National Curriculum, the content of these books was English history from 'the beginning to the end', that is, about 1945! These books are factual outline accounts of what happened, presented chronologically and supported by artists' impressions. They are still useful as a ready source of traditional information, which many schools have kept.

References

Blisten, E. (1997) *Stories from Dickens*, London: Orion Childrens' Books.
Blyth, J. (1992) *Tudor and Stuart Times*, London: Ginn.

Blyth, J. and Hughes, P. (1997) *Using Written Sources in Primary History*, London: Hodder and Stoughton.

Bradbury, J. (1990) *Shakespeare and His Theatre*, New York: Longman.

Brownjohn, S. (1998) *Spotlight on the Victorians*, London: Hodder and Stoughton.

Brownjohn, S. and Gwyn-Jones, G. (1992) *Spotlight on Shakespeare*, London: Hodder and Stoughton (see also teachers' book).

Department for Education (DfE) (1995) *History in the National Curriculum*, London: HMSO.

Emmison, E.G. (1967) *How to Read Local Archives: 1550–1700*, London: Historical Association.

Fines, J. and Nichol, J. (1997) *Teaching Primary History*, London: Heinemann, ch. 8.

Millward, J.S. (ed.) (1961) *The Sixteenth Century: Portraits and Documents*, Oxford: Hutchinson.

Nicolson, A. (ed.) (1988) *The Counties of Britain: A Tudor Atlas, by John Speed*, London: Pavilion.

Pound, J. (1962) *The Elizabethan Corporation of Norwich, 1558–1603*, MA thesis, Birmingham University.

Pound, J. (1977) *Poverty and Vagrancy in Tudor England*, London: Longman.

Reeves, M. (1990) *Elizabethan Citizen*, London: Addison-Wesley Longman.

School Curriculum and Assessment Authority (SCAA) (1997) *History and the Use of Language*, London: SCAA Publications.

Shuter, J. (1996a) *The Poor in Tudor England*, Oxford: Heinemann.

Shuter, J. (1996b) *Shakespeare and the Theatre*, Oxford: Heinemann.

Speed, P.M. (1987) *The Poor and the Wicked: The Elizabethan Age*, Oxford: Oxford University Press.

Tawney, R.H. and Power, E.E. (eds) ([1924] 1951) *Tudor Economic Documents*, London: Longman.

Turner, D. (1985) *William Shakespeare*, London: Wayland.

West, J. (1982) *Village Records*, Chichester, Sussex: Phillimore.

West, J. (1983) *Town Records*, Chichester, Sussex: Phillimore.

William Shakespeare (1981) Loughborough, Leics.: Ladybird Books.

10

LEARNING THE LANGUAGE OF HISTORY

Teaching subject-specific language and concepts

John Sampson, Liz Grugeon and Eleni Yiannaki

Introduction

This chapter, based on the work of a research team at De Montfort University, focuses on the language demands of history in the primary curriculum. Analysis of a single lesson provides some evidence of the way a teacher responds to the requirements of the National Curriculum for both history and English. The research is concerned to examine the extent to which children become aware of and able to use not only the specialist vocabulary of history but also the discursive practices that characterise a particular discipline, that is, how they come to think and behave as historians. Hence, it is concerned with exploring how children learn concepts and terminology that relate to specific subject knowledge (for example, barter, trade, slave) as well as the concepts that underpin historical understanding (in this case, evidence and change). Therefore the questions that the research team are asking include:

- To what extent does subject knowledge and understanding involve using the discourse of a particular discipline?
- To what extent do pupils need to use appropriate language in order to move from everyday commonsense understanding to more explicit knowledge of a subject, using both oral and written modes?

In this chapter we shall look at specific links between the teaching of history and English National Curriculum requirements. The undoubted benefits of literature and narrative will be discussed elsewhere. Our concern here is to examine the extent to which the discourse of history has to be taught and learned before the learner can be said to have a satisfactory grasp of subject knowledge, as described in the history Study Units, so that they are able, 'to communicate their knowledge and understanding of history in a variety of ways, including structured narratives and descriptions' (DfE 1995a: 5). Our research looks at ways in which pupils become able to handle aspects of the discourse that is particular to history, in their talk, reading and writing.

Research in Australian schools in the 1980s and 1990s (Christie 1989; Derewianka 1991; Gibbons 1995) has suggested that in the primary years teachers have been too reliant on the 'recount' genre – that is, the use of a narrative structure in pupils' writing. More recent research in the UK has suggested that pupils do not have an explicit understanding or experience of the different genres they may be asked to use other than narrative (Davies 1996). However, the National Curriculum English Orders (DfE 1995b: 15) are quite explicit, stating that at Key Stage 2: 'Pupils should be given opportunities to write for varied purposes . . . They should be taught to use writing as a means of developing, organising and communicating ideas . . . The forms in which they write should include non-fiction e.g. *reports, instructions, explanations, notes, letters.*' Moreover, 'they should be taught to use features of layout and presentation' (la, 1c). In reading, they are required to 'read and use a wide range of sources of information . . . including information technology-based reference materials, newspapers, encyclopaedias, dictionaries' (1c, ibid.: 13). These orders have clear implications for the teaching of writing in history, as do the requirements for speaking and listening, where 'Pupils should be given opportunities to talk for a range of purposes' (la), many of which seem to be particularly relevant to their development as historians: 'exploring, developing and explaining ideas, planning, predicting and investigating, sharing ideas . . . and opinions, reporting and describing events and observations, presenting to audiences' (1a, ibid.: 11).

More significantly for our study, the English National Curriculum requires that 'Pupils should be taught to organise what they want to say, *and to use vocabulary and syntax that enables the communication of more complex meaning*' (2a, ibid.) and in History in the National Curriculum to 'communicate their knowledge and understanding of history in a variety of ways, including structured narrative and descriptions' (5c, ibid.: 5). Subsequent materials from SCAA (1997a), *Use of Language: A Common Approach*, and a series of subject-specific leaflets have recognised the need to make explicit a common approach to the use of language across the curriculum: for teachers to be aware of the linguistic demands of classroom work. Examples of classroom practice show how teachers can develop pupils' use of language in their teaching of National Curriculum subjects and stress the need for pupils to learn language that is particular to a subject alongside an understanding of grammatical constructions and ways of conveying meaning which may be required for the transmission of that subject knowledge. The SCAA document suggests that 'work in each subject develops specific aspects of pupils' English, since all subjects include demands for specialist concepts and vocabulary and particular uses of written and spoken English' (SCAA 1997a: 6). *History and the Use of Language: Key Stages 1 and 2* (SCAA 1997c) illustrates links between English Programmes of Study and language skills that may be developed in history. *English and the Use of Language Requirements in Other Subjects: Key Stages 1 and 2* (SCAA 1997b) suggests and illustrates areas of the English curriculum which have particular significance in other subjects.

Teaching the language of history

Drawing on research with year 5 classes in two urban middle schools (9–13 year-olds), we have begun to find evidence of the way teachers consciously teach the language of history. Data has been gathered by means of observation and recording of pupil–pupil and pupil–teacher interaction and the collection of relevant written materials. It is being analysed in order to identify ways in which pupils are acquiring and using the language of the subject.

In looking at how Key Stage 2 pupils create meaning in history our analysis has been based on a model derived from the work of Derewianka (1991) which in turn draws on Halliday's (1978) notion of language as social semiotic. This model sees the learning of content in subject disciplines as a continuum from action to reflection. It starts with pupils as 'apprentice' members of a discipline, who have a tentative grasp of the subject and may be helped to develop into confident independent learning. Our interest is to observe and suggest when and how teachers may intervene to offer explicit models which will move pupils on from a basis of personal experience to knowledge of the discourse of the discipline which will enable them to articulate their understanding in a way that is appropriate to the demands of the task within the curriculum area.

Teachers are aware of the need to encourage pupils to organise their writing in different ways that will be 'helpful to the purpose, task and reader' (DfE, 1995b: 9), and that during Key Stage 2 pupils should become increasingly able to handle a range of genre which includes recount, report, explanation, exposition and discussion. In speaking and listening, they should be increasingly able to handle a similar range of purposes; indeed it is through classroom talk that they will first begin to use the 'vocabulary and syntax that enables the communication of more complex meanings' (ibid.: 11). The National Curriculum recognises that it is through talk which is 'exploratory and tentative' (ibid.) that they will first be able to shape their ideas and move towards more 'reasoned, evaluative comments as discussion moves to conclusion' (ibid.: 1) It is in this preliminary talk that they will begin to identify and use different and appropriate features of the discourse required by a particular subject.

Research evidence

The history texts that pupils read will naturally extend the range of genres that they are beginning to become aware of and that they will need to use in their own writing. These will introduce them to specialist terminology and, importantly, to unfamiliar syntax and organisational features. Reading such texts will contribute not only to their knowledge of the topic but to the ways in which they may present ideas about the topic.

Initial analysis of the data in this ongoing research has begun to provide some interesting evidence of the way in which teachers consciously teach the language of a particular discipline and how children seem to use it for themselves. Our first example is drawn from a recording made while a year 5 class were learning about the Ancient Egyptians. If we look at the way the teacher is introducing the class to the particular language they will need to use in order to understand the topic, we could say that the teacher's concerns appear to be twofold:

- the children's precise and accurate use of language:
  Teacher: What is it called when you ask for something?
- the introduction of subject specific terminology:
  Teacher: Has anyone come across the word for making a mummy?

At the same time, they are also being encouraged to use structures which typify the non-fiction texts that they will be required to read and write:

Teacher: Somebody tell me something about the gods.

The pupils' answers show that they are able to use appropriate structures:

> Most of the gods had something they were the leader of.
> To kill a cat in Egypt meant certain death.
> The gods were like a family.

They are beginning to generalise and thus able to construct meaning in an objective way: a way that is closer to the writing they will be required to do in order to record what they are learning about ancient Egyptian civilisation.

In another lesson observed later in the research, the same class are studying the Aztecs. This lesson has provided data which will help to identify some of the characteristics of the teaching and learning of history at Key Stage 2 and to highlight some of the issues that we hope to explore in other contexts and more depth as the research progresses.

The context of the lesson

The interaction between the teacher and the children occurs within a particular sociocultural setting. The contextual features of this setting include:

Time

The history lesson occurred in the latter half of the week – history was scheduled for Thursdays and Fridays – at the end of the day. The data were recorded during the summer term, at the end of the academic year. The teacher's approach during the lesson and the children's responses were quite relaxed and conveyed the impression that all were aware that the school year was drawing to a close.

Participants

The subject teacher on this occasion was also the children's form tutor. This dual role meant that children and teacher, who had spent a lot of time together during the year, were generally on good terms and addressed each other with a certain familiarity. In addition, the researcher had been present in the classroom since the start of the academic year and both teacher and children felt at ease with her.

Nature of the interaction

The lesson, a teacher-led consideration of the Aztecs, sought to distinguish between what constituted a 'primary' and 'secondary' source.

Reason for the interaction

The lesson was undertaken with the intention by the teacher of developing the children's subject knowledge and appreciation of historical understanding. This particular topic had been chosen in accordance with National Curriculum requirements for history at Key Stage 2. This document explicitly influenced what was to be taught and implicitly suggests how it should be undertaken.

Location

The history lesson, of a specific duration, took place in a middle school classroom. The school combined both upper primary and lower secondary years. One feature of this arrangement was that lessons in the school tended to follow a secondary rather than a primary model in the way in which the subject material was presented. The school was generally middle class and multicultural. It was located in a suburban area of a town of medium size in the south-east of England.

Primary sources: using evidence

Unless children understand the nature of sources they will be unable to engage in the process of being historians. The importance of providing 'opportunities to . . . learn about the past from a range of sources of information' (DfE 1995a) is a fundamental part of the National Curriculum for history. In the following extract the teacher is ensuring that the class know what a primary source is – particularly that it is evidence about the people from their time. He makes it clear that this is a *skill* that they will need to develop. Throughout the lesson the teacher uses questioning to elicit the children's knowledge and understanding of the historical process:

Teacher: OK. One of the skills you need in history is to use your eyes when you're looking at evidence. Now can anyone remember what a primary source is? We did this earlier in the year, a primary source? E?

E: Is it something that's the original one?

And to ask for clarification of particular points:

Teacher: Yes, can anybody add any detail to that? Something that's the original one, she said. K?

He continues to encourage them to add to their definition of what they mean by a primary source until, together, they reach the definition he is seeking. In asking for their definition, he uses, and encourages the children to use, vocabulary that is appropriate for the task: original, evidence, skills, definition, conclusions:

K: Is it like if you have a statue and the statue . . . something like that is the primary source?

Teacher: Right, good. E, have you got anything to add to that?

E: It's when it's the original one, not a fake one.

Teacher: Yes, certainly it's not a fake, something to do with time maybe . . . something to do with the time of it, when it was made . . . S?

S: It's from the time when it was made.

Teacher: It's from the time when it was made? Yes, I know what you mean. Yes, K?

K: It's been made in the same time as the people that you're looking at.

The teacher encourages them to ask questions and to try out and share ways of expressing a definition of what they understand by primary source. Once they have collaborated to reach a satisfactory or more specific definition, he reinforces this by providing a more precise version which he elaborates on:

Teacher: Absolutely right . . . it's something that dates from the time that you're actually studying, so if you're studying Aztec civilisation 700 years ago and you've got a statue that's about 700 years, made by the Aztecs, that is a primary source, it's an important piece of evidence that you can look at very closely and perhaps draw some conclusions about.

Once they have reached a definition, he states what is to be the focus of the lesson which follows. He goes on to remind them about the process of using evidence, that it leads to conclusions, however hypothetical, and he then goes on to point out the problems of validity and reliability that have to be considered when using evidence:

Teacher: Supposing the only statue we have of Coatlicue was that one that's shown on page 28, could we learn anything really definitive about the Aztec people if we only had that one statue?

The teacher speculates upon historical situations to further explore the notion of reliability of evidence and invites the children to do likewise:

Teacher: I mean, it's unlikely, but that statue could have been made by one person who was living in a cave all by himself, couldn't it, or it might have been made by the king's own sculptor . . . you wouldn't know, would you, from one statue . . . Supposing we found ten statues of Coatlicue in different parts of the Aztec empire and they all looked roughly alike, what would that prove?

The children respond by drawing conclusions:

B: It would prove that in every part of the empire, they're still praising the same god.
Teacher: Very good, it proved that they praised the same god, absolutely right. S?
S: And they thought that the gods looked exactly alike.
Teacher: Absolutely right. They all had the same idea of what the god looked like, so you know that there's good communication throughout the empire and that the priests are telling the people what the gods looked like.

Having established the key concepts of primary source materials he can then use a similar process to reach a definition of a secondary source:

Teacher: So this is a primary source. What's a secondary source, D?
D: Is that a source that's been made by humans about the past?
Teacher: Yes, that's pretty good, it's a source that's been made by humans about the past. OK, we've got one here *(holding up a book)* this book is a secondary source, it's a book written by people who've done a lot of research about the Aztecs. This is a secondary source.

Developing enquiry skills

Having established that the children understand the difference between primary and secondary sources the teacher returns to the skills that they will need to handle different sources:

Teacher: Right, I've said that one of the skills you need in history is the skill of observation. Can you take a look at the statue of Coatlicue and I'd like you to describe the features of it. You've already been drawing it, I want some words now. Could somebody tell me something about it, yes?
S: It's got two heads
Teacher: Try and give me a bit more detail . . .

He has moved on to develop the children's skills in using a piece of historical evidence, in this case, a photograph of an Aztec artefact. He accepts their answers but is trying to extend them, encouraging them to look more closely and describe what they see more precisely, to examine the evidence and draw conclusions:

Teacher: How many hands are on the necklace? Yes?
S: Four
Teacher: Four, very good, there are four hands on the necklace. Right, can someone tell me something about the hands . . . you're looking at the hands on the necklace around Coatlicue's neck.
S: They look like human hands.
Teacher: Pretty good, they're human hands.
K: The top two hands are either side and one pair of hands are on the bottom there.
Teacher: Very good.
S: How do you know that?

At this point, the teacher is challenged by a child who is unconvinced by the conclusions being drawn and asks for justification, showing that the children are beginning to understand that you can question, justify and interpret. He continues to encourage the children to scrutinise the evidence by asking questions: 'Right, something else about the statue?' 'What do you think they are?' The children discuss whether what they can see might be teeth or tongues. The teacher sums up by re-emphasising the provisional nature of the conclusions that they are drawing:

Teacher: All right, if you were describing this, no one expects you to be certain about everything, so you could just say, 'Below the fangs of the snake there are two very large fangs or tongues.' We're looking at a picture and describing what we can see and how these things are fangs or tongues.

He proceeds then to illustrate the limitations of this kind of evidence: the children are challenged to attempt to answer an impossible question:

Teacher: Does this picture tell us how big the statue is?
Children: No!
Teacher: No, and that is a problem, isn't it. I'm afraid that the book lets us down a bit there.

He spends some time encouraging them to explore the possible scale of this statue and to justify their opinions:

Teacher: Who reckons it might be as big as the blackboard? What we need is to do some research about it and we could find out. Could you give us any reason why you think that?
S: It's big.
Teacher: But we don't know how big they are.
D: It could be a church one and they pray to it.
Teacher: Very good and then you'd expect that to be big, wouldn't you. Yes?
S: 'Cos people can look at it.
Teacher: Yes, I think it's probably bigger to make people look at it and worship it and, of course, it's meant to be quite frightening as well.
S: Because it was quite important to the Aztecs it was made quite big.

He encourages a number of children to speculate about reasons for the statue being a large one but also wants them to consider that it might be very small, drawing an analogy with 'something that's very important in our civilisation'. E suggests, 'Jesus on the cross', something small enough to wear around the neck; the teacher agrees but makes them look again to establish whether there is evidence to support an assumption that this is, in fact, a very large statue:

K: I think it's quite big because I would have thought of the temples as being quite big, like if you walk into a church then there's all the pictures there at the front.

Teacher: Yes, it looks as if it's meant to be stared at from a distance, doesn't it. The only hint that I can see is the amount of detail in the carving, if you look at the amount of carving around the head that looks to me as if it was done with a hammer and chisel. If it was really tiny you couldn't get all that detail in.

In these extracts from this lesson, we can see how the teacher engages the children in the process of dealing with historical evidence, encouraging them to observe closely, speculate and hypothesise about what they can see, to provide justification for their assertions, to see and begin to use appropriate specialist terminology and to talk about this.

Change

Later in the same lesson the teacher explores another key concept. As he encourages them to consider similarity and difference he begins to focus a little on the key element of change by comparing trade and the rules governing trade. The children have identified one of the people in an illustration of an Aztec market place in the book they are reading (Kent *et al.* 1993):

Teacher: Now who is the person in the big cloak, what's he saying? J, can you read what he is saying, please?

J: *(reading)* Let me see if this is good enough for me to sell in the market.

Teacher: Yes, so what is he doing?

S: Is he the market inspector?

The teacher draws an analogy between the presence of the market inspector and the effect of a police car on the motorway. He asks what might happen to the boy in the picture who has broken an egg and they agree that he would not be killed. The teacher then draws on his own knowledge and evidence to support this:

Teacher: There's lots of evidence in books that the Aztecs wrote, that they loved their children and did their best to bring them up properly.

In this way he reminds them that there are other sources than the ones they were able to identify earlier; different versions provided by 'lots of evidence in books'. He also encourages them to speculate about ways in which the role of the market inspector would be similar to that of a trading standards officer today.

Developing the children's understanding of specific terminology/concepts and subject knowledge

Having completed a drawing of the statue in their exercise books, the children read aloud from the illustrated page 'The Market' (in Kent *et al.* 1993). Referring to this text, he offers more specific information, explanation and clarification:

Teacher: You've seen it before, it's all about the Aztec market *(he reads from the page)* 'Every five days a great market was held at Tenochtitlan. People came from miles around.'

They have seen this before and he is reminding them about material they have discussed earlier in the term:

Teacher: Because the Aztecs were such good fighters they were able to subdue all the tribes around them and build up an empire, remember, they would fight against other tribes and when they beat them, they didn't burn all their villages and kill all the men, like some armies have in the past. They would say: 'We are going to leave you to get on with your lives but every year you're going to hand over to us a lot of the best things that you have made . . .' and that's how the Aztec empire got rich.

Here the teacher is clarifying and reinforcing their understanding of the concept of empire, using quite specific terms, *tribes, subdue, empire,* and drawing attention to the particular way in which the Aztecs did this, not 'like some armies have in the past'. He deals with the concept of bartering which is illustrated in the text: 'People used to come there for market day and you could swap things, they didn't use money, they basically swapped things.' As the children look at this text he attempts to contextualise the culture, encouraging them to focus on what is familiar and what is different, identifying cultural differences. The fact that turquoise was worth more than gold to the Aztecs is an interesting difference:

Teacher: If you offered an Aztec person a piece of gold and a piece of turquoise the same size, they would have no hesitation in taking the turquoise. Of course, now, in our civilisation, turquoise has very little value, everybody wants the gold.

He explains the presence of slaves for sale in the market and the reason for the restraints they are wearing, establishing that the children know how the slaves come to be there:

Teacher: Where did those slaves come from?

S: The wars.
T: Yes, they were captured during the wars.

As they look at this page the teacher is able to clarify a number of concepts and provide further information as he revises ground that they have already covered. As he does this he is also providing vocabulary and syntax that they will draw on when they come to write about the Aztec civilisation for themselves.

The organisation and communication of new ideas

Many of the lessons observed involved a practical activity which would be undertaken in small groups or individually and would involve writing. The purpose of the writing would be to reinforce what had already been discussed, to affirm the understanding of concepts and language explored in the lesson. The lessons had a similar structure which involved the children in using language in a variety of ways, all of which related to their acquisition of different aspects of the history curriculum: they used language to demonstrate their knowledge and understanding of the subject area; responded to the teacher's questions; questioned and often reshaped his and their own ideas during the course of any discussion. And often, as a final process of reshaping, they produced, either collaboratively or individually, an account of their new understanding. One child wrote:

A written description of Coatlicue

Coatlicue has 2 serpent heads and a necklace with heads, hearts and hands. Notice how they all begin with 'h'. For legs and arms she has snakes. The hands on the necklace are right and left and are cut off at the wrists. In between the human hands there are hearts and at the bottom of the necklace, there is a human skull.

Throughout the process illustrated in this brief account of a single lesson, it can be seen how the teacher constantly involves the children in ways of behaving like historians and models ways in which they will be expected to present their understanding and knowledge.

Conclusion

Returning to the questions that the research team are asking, it seems that the evidence provided by an analysis of a single lesson shows that, through

Figure 10.1 Coatlicue, Goddess of the Earth

careful questioning and explanation, key concepts and subject specific terminology can be taught. This confirms the work carried out by Cooper (1992).

The lesson analysed also begins to illustrate ways in which teachers may introduce pupils to the particular language required by the study of history and enable them to use appropriate language as they move from everyday commonsense understanding to handling the Key Elements alongside particular Study Units. It indicates how they come to think and behave as historians.

References

Christie, F. (1989) *Language Education*, Oxford: Oxford University Press.

Cooper, H. (1992) *The Teaching of History: Implementing the National Curriculum*, London: David Fulton.

Davies, C. (1996) 'The Understandings and Experience of Writing Across the Curriculum of Year 6 Pupils: Work in Progress', paper presented at the Universities Council for the Education of Teachers (UCET) Conference, 16 November.

Department for Education (DfE) (1995a) *History in the National Curriculum*, London: HMSO.

—— (1995b) *English in the National Curriculum*, London: HMSO.

Derewianka, B. (1991) 'Rocks in the Head: Children and the Language of Geology', in R. Carter (ed.), *Knowledge about Language about the Curriculum*, London: Hodder and Stoughton.

Gibbons, P. (1995) *Learning a New Register in a Second Language: The Role of Teacher/Student Talk*, Working Papers in Language and Literacy no. 1, Centre for Language and Literacy, Sydney: University of Technology.

Halliday, M.A.K. (1978) *Language as a Social Semiotic: The Social Interpretation of Language and Meaning*, London: Edward Arnold.

Kent, P., Casson, C. and Middleton, G. (1993) *Exploration and Encounters*, Hemel Hempstead, Herts.: Simon and Schuster Educational.

School Curriculum and Assessment Authority (SCAA) (1997a) *Use of Language: A Common Approach*, London: SCAA Publications.

—— (1997b) *English and the Use of Language Requirement in Other Subjects: Key Stages 1 and 2*, London: SCAA Publications.

—— (1997c) *History and the Use of Language: Key Stages 1 and 2*, London: SCAA Publications.

11

WRITING ABOUT HISTORY
IN THE EARLY YEARS

Hilary Cooper

If we are not proactive in demonstrating that convincing and precise links can be established in planning and assessing history and English, particularly at Key Stage 1, we are in danger of having a very narrow and impoverished curriculum imposed on us. The writing, so to speak, is on the wall! Judith O'Reilley sounded a warning note as long ago as 23 February 1997 (the *Sunday Times*, 2): 'At present it is left to schools to decide how much time they devote to reading and writing. However, Labour believes it is too often taught through other subjects such as history or project work.' Yet we should be confident in our defence of Key Stage 1 history, for the tide could be about to turn. Several large-scale international studies are demonstrating that a narrow literacy and numeracy skills based curriculum fails to transmit the cultural values which underpin our society and, moreover, that there is no direct causal link between pedagogy, attainment in literacy and national economic competitiveness. They are also showing that it is a mistake to try to upgrade literacy and numeracy standards by downgrading the rest of the curriculum. One such study is Professor Robin Alexander's recent research on primary schooling in England, France, Russia, India and the United States, which challenges the core assumptions underpinning the current drive for higher educational standards. Professor Alexander has restated the view that the values underlying Britain's current obsession with literacy and numeracy targets are the same now as they were in the 1870s: 'economic instrumentalism, cultural reproduction and social control' and that 'as educationalists we have to challenge them' (*The Times Education Supplement*, 5 December 1997, 17). This chapter describes a case study which was a modest attempt to do this.

The chapter explores ways in which children's writing can be developed through history at Key Stage 1. History provides contexts for developing the skills of punctuation, spelling, handwriting and structuring for a range of purposes in response to a variety of stimuli. There are opportunities to ask and to try to answer questions about the past. These may be communicated as single words at level 1 (lists, labels, names); as sentences at level 2a (captions, notes, rules, instructions); as sequences of sentences at level 2b (picture-stories, quizzes, questionnaires, speech bubbles, accounts, descriptions, deductions, explanations), and in more varied forms at level 3 (plays, songs, poems, letters, reports). Indeed, SCAA (1995) recommended continuing work in English linked to blocks of work in history. This is essential time management if the National Curriculum aspirations for breadth, depth and progression and an introduction to the thinking process which lies at the heart of each subject are to be achieved at Key Stage 1. And yet it appears that few teachers 'risk' setting non-fiction writing, although able Key Stage 1 writers 'do well when they attempt genres other than story' (SCAA 1997a: 11).

Five BA (Qualified Teacher Status: QTS) students volunteered to work intensively for three days with Pat Etches and her class of year 1/2 children at Stramongate School, in Kendal, to investigate possible links between history and writing through finding out about life in Kendal Castle 'a long time ago'. This theme was part of the school's medium-term plan for humanities. Pat seized on an opportunity which arose the week before the students' visit to introduce the idea of castles. Some children had performed badly on a Standard Attainment Task on fractions so Pat told then the story of a king and queen who could not agree whether their castle flag should be red or yellow; the children had to help by designing on squared paper a variety of flags which were half red and half yellow. The king and queen were so pleased with the flags that they had a banquet to celebrate but could not divide the food equally. The following Friday afternoon at 'choosing time' a group of children chose to make a wonderful box castle, complete with mound, moat, drawbridge and battlements. The project had begun!

Next week the students arrived. On the first morning they worked with groups of children to establish what they already knew about castles. First, each child made a concept map. This session was followed by a whole-class brainstorm to decide what the children still wanted to know. In the afternoon we went to the castle to try to find out some of the answers. During day 2 and the morning of day 3 (five 1½ hour sessions) the students worked with all the children in five rotating groups.

Each student planned a sequence of activities to help children find out from books what could not be learned from the site. On the final afternoon the group work was collated in written form by making information boards for children about the castle, (the children said the boards at the site were a bit difficult), and through a reconstruction of a feast at the castle.

Concept maps: what do we know about castles?

All the children were asked to imagine 'their' castle, draw a picture of it and write on it everything they knew about life in castles long ago. The students supported by scribing or spelling when asked and sometimes by questioning. This activity provided simultaneous learning objectives and assessment opportunities for history and writing.

History

* *Learning objectives*:
  Children will remember and record the range and depth of their existing knowledge about life in castles (Key Element (KE) 2), indicate an under-standing that it was different from the present (KE2c) and communicate this through drawing and labelling (KE5).
* *Assessment opportunity*:
  The child's concept map recognises a distinction between past and present (level 1). The concept map includes factual knowledge about how life in a castle was different from life today (level 2).

Writing

* *Learning objective*:
  Children will remember and organise their ideas and information about life in castles and communicate them in writing (1a, b).
* *Assessment opportunity*:
  The child can, with support/independently, record information as labels level 1), as sentences (level 2).

All the children had a concept of a castle as a big strong building with battlements, standing on a hill and with a moat. (Kendal Castle was after all close to the school). Many understood that everyday life in a castle was different from life today. A castle was a defensive building where knights might fight, and was protected by a guarded drawbridge. However, it was interesting that the amount of detail in the pictures, which was evidence of children's factual knowledge of how life in a castle was different from today, (stables, horse, a well, a fishpond, a portcullis, arrow slits, dungeons, clothes), roughly mirrored their writing level (see Figure 11.1). At the beginning of the continuum children drew little relevant detail and wrote only one or two words. Often there was a delightful fantasy element: garlands of flowers around the towers, or Max (from *Where the Wild Things Are*: Sendak 1970) in his boat at night on a rescue mission. However, there were also suggestions that such children were trying to move beyond the fantasy: M's picture, which included smiling birds and butterflies and the words 'queen', 'king' and 'guards', was supplemented by scribed references to knights fighting, horses to ride on, goats, water to drink, a drawbridge and dungeons. Children knew that this was a description of life a long time ago, (expressed with difficulty as 'more than six years ago' or 'a hundred years

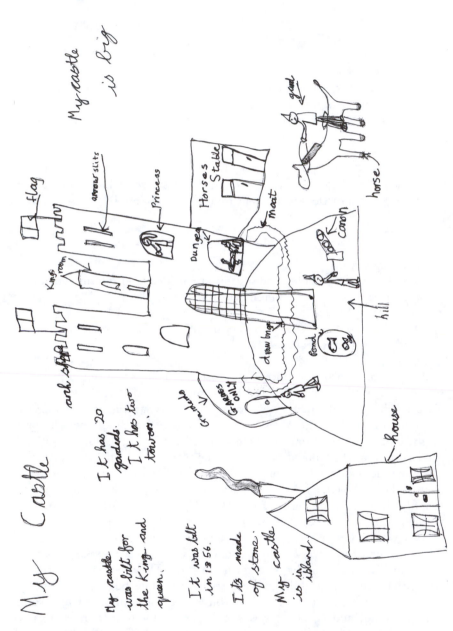

Figure 11.1 Concept map

old'). At the other end of the continuum children had more detailed know-ledge of how life in the castle was different. This was conveyed through a combination of single words, labels, often specialised concepts (enemy, kingdom, village, servants, hall), and sentences: 'The castle has got thin windows'; 'It has got a drawbridge'; 'It is made of stone'. These children too knew that the castle was very old, and that time can be measured in precise four-digit numbers (these ranged from '1797' to '8,000 years old' – almost accurate!).

Kendal Castle: what do we want to find out?

KE4 ask questions about the past. The class shared their concept maps of castles then brainstormed questions they wanted to investigate on their visit to Kendal Castle. Pat Etches recorded these on a flip chart:

> How big is it?
> What is it made of? How was it built? Why?
> How did they defend it? [sic]
> How high is the hill? Was there a moat?
> How did they cook their food?
> Where would they get water from?
> Where did the king and queen eat? Sleep?
> Where did the soldiers sleep?
> Where did the horses live?
> What would it look like in the old days?

The children's questions were structured over lunchtime into five focuses, one for each group:

* *Now and then*:

    What can you see from the castle now?
    What could you have seen 'then': for certain? perhaps?

* *Attacking the castle*:

    Why was the castle built here?
    How could you attack? Where?
    What might you see? hear?

- *Daily life*:

  Where did they store food? What food?
  Where was the great hall? What might it be like to feast there?
  How did they cook? wash? keep warm? get water?

- *Survey of site*:
  Two groups were engaged on this focus, meeting where there is evidence in the wall of two gangs of workmen meeting.

  Measure curtain-wall, windows, doorways.
  Note materials; where did they come from? How?

Visit to Kendal Castle: finding out from a site

The visit, like the concept maps, provided simultaneous learning objectives and assessment opportunities for history and for writing.

History

- *Learning objective*:
  Children will try to answer some of their brainstorm questions about Kendal Castle using the site as a source of information (KE4) (supplemented by computerised reconstructions on information boards – KE3).
- *Assessment opportunity*:
  Children can find out answers to some of their questions through observations and deductions on site.

Writing

- *Learning objective*:
  Children will begin to understand the value of writing notes (1c) as a means of remembering ideas and information (1a), using the castle site as a stimulus (1b).
- *Assessment opportunity*:
  The child can record answers to questions as a sketch with scribed note; as a sketch and single word; as sentence(s).

The children recorded what they observed, and in some cases added notes about what the castle might have been like in the past. Some of

162

the drawings/records made by the youngest children were painstakingly observed and remarkably accurate: a broken tower; a window; the shapes of stones in the wall; there were remarkable developments of the stereotypical images produced in the morning. The surveying group used string, metre sticks, tapes and paces to estimate and measure. Their notes record that it is '350 giant strides to the top of the mound – very hard with armour'; the fireplace is 1.6 m; dungeon window 2 m thick and 30 cm high; 'outside wall by kitchen 4 m thick'; well 2 m across. S made a careful drawing of a barred window labelled 'the bars' and also drawings labelled 'tolet', 'chimey' and 'fire' (Figure 11.2(i)). Older children wrote lists going beyond the information observed, with descriptive notes of what the place felt like ('dungeon scary, ghostly, very dark, smelly'); how it might have been used ('cellar, stone shelves – big wooden crates, they put it down here to keep fresh'. Also, 'Well to get washed they splashed themselves with water; great hall, eat up hear, food, fish, partys, important friends, entertainment, banquits. A large fire would have kept them warm' (Figure 11.2(ii)).

What else do we want to know? Artefacts, pictures and information books (KE4)

When the children arrived in school on day 2 it was clear that their enthusiasm had been fired and they wanted to find out more about castles. P brought in a pile of books; he had found out what musical instruments might have been played in the castle and what the beds might have looked like. T had drawn plans at home for a shield and a sword 'to make today'. He had thought about how to protect his hand ('It's quite tiring making designs'). Someone else had brought a book to school for the first time ever – about fairy tales and a castle with a magically long winding staircase. The five sequences of activities the students had planned were off to a good start.

Finding out about the past from brasses: Sarra Thorne

Sarra Thorne based her activities on a selection of replica medieval brasses from the college collection, including one of Catherine Parr, who had lived in Kendal Castle as a child, to help children investigate what the people who lived in the castle may have looked like. The first two activities which Sarra planned are practical and focus on history: using the brasses to find out about and communicate observations about the past. The discussion, the speaking and listening which was central to these activities informed the two writing tasks which followed. These have concurrent history and writing learning objectives and assessment opportunities. Before the first group of children arrived the brasses had been covered with paper – a mystery. Children were asked to rub a tiny area very carefully with the gold or silver crayons to see

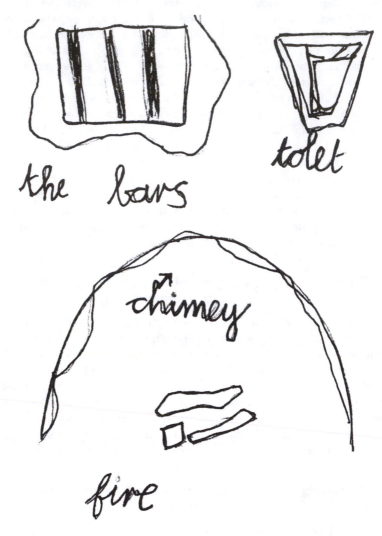

Figure 11.2(i) Notes on site (level 1)

what would happen – magic. They described each part as it emerged, often revising their guesses as new or as contradictory evidence appeared: 'It's a ship . . . no it's a crown . . . it's a king . . . no he's carrying the crown . . . he might be a servant.'

They described each detail: 'She's praying . . . two rings . . . fur on her wrist . . . a thoughtful expression . . . a flower necklace . . . a squirrel-like animal at the bottom of her dress . . . a hat under her head-dress, it keeps her head-dress up . . . a lovely long belt . . . her dress has folds in it.'

164

Kendal Castle

Dungeon
  teary
    ghostly
    very dark
    smelly
        great hall
          eat food
            fish
              potatoes
                partys
                  entertainment
                    banquet.
              A large fire would
              have kept them warm.

              cellar
            on stone shelves.
            they put it down
            here to keep fresh.

                Well
            get water for washing
                and drinking.

Figure 11.2(ii) Notes on site (level 2)

They also made deductions and inferences and considered possibilities: 'He's got a long sword . . . to protect himself . . . stirrups . . . he must ride a horse . . . chain down his legs and arms . . . and chain round his face . . . so he can move around *and* protect himself . . . on his flag shield he has a upside-down v shape . . . I think that is a special sign.'

Sometimes children's deductions were challenged: 'A suit of armour . . . a metal, tin suit . . . so they don't get killed with bullets'. 'Did they have bullets then?' After some thought: 'Well, they had gunpowder in Guy Fawkes time . . . so they probably only had swords when he was a knight.'

When the rubbings were completed the children noticed how the clothes were not all the same: 'different shapes of head-dress'; 'some dressed plainer than others'; 'not all the same style of armour or weapons'. Sarra helped them to consider why: 'different times', 'some were richer'.

Communicating observations from brasses

When the next group worked with the brasses they each chose their favourite article of dress, jewellery or armour and made a replica, carefully observing and recording the details: a head-dress, a crown, a necklace, a sword. Observation and description were scrupulous and the replication resourceful (although accuracy was difficult for a six-year-old to achieve with a collection of beads, lace, card and foil).

Communicating understanding of 'now' and 'then' from brasses

History

- *Learning objective*:
  To identify differences between clothes now and then (KE2c).

Writing

- *Learning objective*:
  To organise information (1a) in the form of lists (1c), using the brasses as a stimulus (1b).

Some of the children found it difficult to say how the lord or lady on the brass looked different from people today; they tended to describe one and then the other, or not to compare specific aspects of clothing. To help them structure their ideas Sarra asked them first to draw a picture of their mum or dad. They folded a piece of A4 paper in half, labelled 'then' and 'now' and listed direct comparisons. This format successfully structured their embryonic thinking about similarities and differences, although these tended to be closed does/not comparisons: wearing a long dress, wearing a short dress; she is praying, she is not praying; she looks sad, she looks happy. However, through discussion, while making the lists children began to consider the reasons for some of the differences: 'she looks thoughtful because she is praying' – or 'because she is dead'.

Communicating observations, deductions and inferences from brasses through extended writing

History

- *Learning objective*:
  To make deductions and inferences about brasses (KE4).
- *Assessment opportunity*:
  Child demonstrates ability to find out about the past from the brass (level 1); begins to answer questions (level 2); goes beyond single observations to record these in extended writing (2a–e).

Writing

Following the discussion of the brasses with Sarra and Pat, about a third of the class were able to produce a piece of extended writing, interpreting the brasses as an historical source. This provided a good example of the interdependence of writing and the development of historical thinking. First, writing skills, punctuation, spelling and handwriting can be developed and assessed in the context of writing about an historical source. But more importantly, it is also possible to help children develop a sense of structure through developing the historical process of description, followed by inference and the weighing of possibilities, in order to reach a conclusion. This structure requires the development of specialised vocabulary and also of complex sentence structure in order to express probabilistic ideas (I think, perhaps), and to make causal connections (therefore, because). The relationship between the development of structured writing and of historical thinking is illustrated in the following examples.

K attempts to use recently learned special vocabulary (knight, guard, battle), and struggles when this is not remembered; the knight in armour wears 'a big hat'. She uses 'because' and 'so' and probabilistic vocabulary ('I think') but there is no structure of description, deduction based on evidence and conclusion; therefore the writing rambles on:

> I think he lives in a castle he lives in a castle because he wud have to guard it because men wud get in the castle so thats why the knight had to stay in the carstle.

My rubbing is a knight who lived
a long time a go. He has a
shield and a sword to protect
him self. He is wearing chain
down his legs and arms and
chain round his face. He is
standing on a lion and I think
he looks thought ful. He is
wearing chain because so
he can move about easly
and to protect himself. I think
he rides a horse and gos out
fighting. I think he lives in a
castle. On his flag shield he
has a up side down v shape I
think that is his special
sign.

Figure 11.3(i) Deductions from brasses: extended writing

By contrast A and P each produced a structured piece of writing which reflected the process of historical thinking. They begin with a strong over-arching statement saying who they are writing about:

A: My rubbing is a knight who lived a long time ago.
P: My lady looks like she has a very important family.

They continue with detailed description, and in A's case with some causal explanation:

A: He is wearing a sword to protect himself. He is wearing chain down his

My lady looks like she has a very important family. She has a beautiful dress. On the dress there is some beautiful patens. Round her midl there is a long belt with a tassel on the end. She has got a sort of head-dress on. On the bottem of her dress, there is a squirrel - like animal on the bottem of her dress. A neclas is hanging roun her neck. She has a cross expressio on her face. I think she is praying. I think she lived in a castle, or a grand house. I think she was marred to a king.

Figure 11.3(ii) Deductions from brasses: extended writing

legs and arms and round his face, so he can move easily and protect himself.

P: On the dress there are beautiful patterns, Round her midal there is a long belt with a tussel at the end. She has got a long dress on. On the bottom of her dress there is a squirrel like animal . . .

Next, they offer some possible interpretations of the evidence described:

A: I think he rides a horse and gos out fighting. On his flag shield there's an upside down 'V' shape. I think its a special sign.

P: She has a cross expression. I think she's praying. I think she lived in a castle or a grand house.

They end up with a conclusion:

A: I think he lives in a castle.
P: I think she was married to a king.

What was Catherine Parr really like? Laura Jones

Catherine Parr, sixth wife of King Henry VIII, lived in Kendal Castle as a child. Laura Jones used this opportunity to introduce the children to two different images of Catherine Parr: an engraving of her as a young woman and the National Gallery portrait of her by an unknown artist, dated 1545, when she was in her thirties.

This activity was based on work which Pat Etches had done on Guy Fawkes for the SCAA book on Assessment at Key Stages 1 and 2 (SCAA 1997b).

History

- *Learning objective*:
  Children will understand that two portraits of the same person can convey different and sometimes contradictory information.
- *Assessment opportunity*:
  Children observe differences in clothes, age (level 2); identify differences in mood; attempt to explain the differences (level 3).

Writing

- *Learning objective*:
  Children will structure their ideas about the differences between the portraits of Catherine Parr and the reasons for this (1a/b).

First, Laura asked the children to write down on one half of a piece of paper all that they could tell about Catherine Parr from the engraving: how old she was; what they could work out from her dress; what sort of a person she was. Then she showed them the replica oil painting and asked them to write answers to the same questions about this lady on the second half of the paper. They shared their contrasting ideas about both pictures, then Laura told the children that both pictures were of Catherine Parr and asked why they thought they were so different. A synopsis of their ideas is given in Table 11.1.

Table 11.1 Synopsis of children's responses to two portraits of Catherine Parr

Engraving	*Portrait*
Appearance (clothes; age)	
• Important, rich, because of her gem bracelet necallas on her neck, pearls on her head.	• Very rich, very important her jurly is lovely, rings and necklace.
• She looks like a prinses – isn't maride – not wearing a ring.	• May be a queen.
• Lovely wight coler; headdress, transloocen dress, shiny, looks grand, frills on her sleeves.	• A ring on her third finger – she is maride.
• Wide eyes; beautiful soft skin.	• Stiff collar, on her hat is a plume, and some beads, velvet dress, her sleeves have roses and hearts on it, and floury frills.
• She is a young lady.	• Hard eyes.
	• Old lady.
What sort of a person?	
• She looks helpful, because you can tell by her face.	• I think she would not of minded what her portrait looked like.
• Prity.	• Not happy; sad queen.
• A happy face.	• Thortful.
• Thoughtful.	• Tired.
• Looks like exciting things happened to her.	• Looks cross.
• I think the artist liked her.	• Bad.
	• Mad.
	• Staring.

Why are the portraits different?

Different artists – the second one might not like her.
She was older.
She was richer.
She had had a sad life.

Plan for a medieval banquet: Alex Fisher and Anne Braine

It was decided that on the final afternoon of the project the children would create their interpretation of a medieval banquet (History KE3, 5). This involved research based on artists' illustrations in information books, and original recipes and pictures in *The Medieval Cookbook* (Black 1996). It resulted in a variety of forms of writing. Alex Fisher's groups wrote guest lists, invitations, menus and lists of entertainments to be provided.

The guest lists reflected a blend of recent knowledge and fantasy: 'KingHennryeigHEETH (aka King Henry the arhth), Catherine Parr, a squire, a prinse, a quene, knights, ladies, Baron Dorset, prince Charming and Sant Jorj'. The invitations were in a formal party invitation format familiar to the children (Figure 11.4(i)).

Menus were planned in courses and included deer, squirrels, boar's head, pigeons, rabbit (white meat only), eels, whole fish and eggs in jelly (Figure

To lady Felice
you are invited to
Kendal castle for a
bankwit. It starts at
half past eleven

Love from
queen cathen
par.

Figure 11.4(i) 'Banquet invitation'

11.4(ii)). It was agreed that 'they liked their food to look nice'. The pigeons, the children thought, were probably kept 'in a pen, like doves', or caught with nets. The programmes for entertainment were thoughtfully divided into 'during the meal' ('storys, jesting, lute') and 'after the meal' ('singing, puppets, dancing, magicans, tornaments') (Figure 11.4(iii)). The extension activity was to draw and cut out food for the feast. Miss Fisher provided a feather to decorate the roast peacock and several rather glum-looking boars' heads were prepared.

Ann Braine's groups provided the entertainment. The jesters listed their skills as observed in book illustrations: 'I can jugel. I can mace funny faces. I

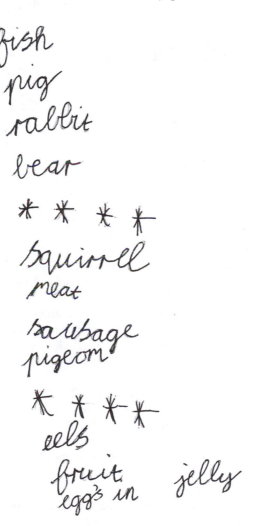

Figure 11.4(ii) 'Banquet menu'

Programme

During the meal -

storys
Jesting
lute.

After the meal - singing
dancing
tornaments

Figure 11.4(iii) 'Banquet entertainment'

can mace sad faces. I can mace som mysic'. They wrote down their jokes, using question marks and speech marks; familiar formats required appropriate modification: 'Why did the chikin cross the drawbridge?' – it is interesting that specially learned spelling was remembered. One group composed songs for a recorder and a drum. Another devised a formal dance to the music of 'Minstrel Songs and Dances for a Medieval Banquet' (a 'Past Times' tape).

The oldest group wrote stories to be read aloud during the banquet: another extended piece of writing which could be assessed for content, structure and key skills. Some stories used vocabulary and sentence structure imaginatively to convey mood and vivid images:

> they had servants running about and food being served, people chattaring, clanging of plates and I forgot story telling, jesters, jokes, jugglers, singing and dancing. Let the Banquet begin!

The structure of these stories was supported by the children's familiarity with fairy tales, which they often mirrored closely:

> Once upon a time in a far away land a king and a queen lived in a castle. One day the queen had a baby daughter. They called her pricess Ross. On Rosses 5th birthday she pricked her finger on a

174

spindell and fell into a deep sleep. Not onley did she fall a sleep but everybody eles in the king dome fell a sleep while they were sleeping a prince came to the castle. He looked around the castle, and then went up to kiss Ross on the lipss.

A skend latter she awoke. Then all the king dome awoke and the prince and Ross lived happy every after.

('Sleeping Beauty': story for banquet)

Information boards: Alex Hayes

History

- *Learning objective*:
  To answer questions about the past (KE4b) and communicate what they had found out from the castle (KE4a), and the computerised reconstructions on information boards at the site (KE3).
- *Assessment opportunity*:
  Comparison of child's initial concept map with plan for information board.

Writing

- *Learning objective*:
  Write labels and captions for key to plan, using special learned vocabulary (1a, b, c, 2b).
- *Assessment opportunity*:
  Child can select, write and spell recently learned special vocabulary correctly.

The children had found that the information boards on the site contained too much writing and were difficult for them to understand, so they agreed with Miss Hayes that it would be a good idea to make simplified boards for other children. They used measurements taken on the visit to draw a scale plan of aspects of the site, made a key (showing, for example, stables, well, church, stocks, fish pond, drawbridge and portcullis) and wrote brief supporting information based on the computerised reconstruction.

The perspectives of the plans varied with maturity, as did the information recorded, but the new display boards and the notes Alex made as she supported the children in making them demonstrated a considerable development from the concept map made only three days earlier.

Everyone wore their brass-rubbing replica clothes to the banquet. The (drawings of) dishes of pike and salmon, hare and venison with pepper sauce, cream tarts and rose pudding were clearly inordinately heavy. The jugglers caught (nearly) all the balls. The stories were listened to with rapt attention, the chicken crossed the drawbridge to gales of laughter. Everyone danced to the viol, the harp and the crumhorn of the Past Times tape, and Baron Dorset looked remarkably like the headmaster – except that he was carrying a lance.

What did the teacher, children and students learn from the project?

The teacher

The teacher, Pat Etches, wrote:

> Covering the requirements of two Orders at once is good time-management but the link between history and English is much more than this. Through spoken and written language the children learned to form and use historical concepts. For example when the children were talking and writing about the brasses they knew what they could *see*, the spurs, the scabbard and so on but they did not have the vocabulary they needed to describe them. The students helped them to learn new words through non-threatening activities, which interested them. It is important that we give children the support and motivation to try out new concepts; we must give them the 'tools for the job' if they are to learn to talk confidently about the past.
>
> English can enhance children's understanding in history. The ground work we did reading stories and setting up role-play situations stimulated their imagination so that they had the *desire* to find out what it was like to live in a castle, how people dressed, what their needs and feelings may have been.
>
> History lends itself so well to developing all the English attainment targets: speaking and listening, particularly by prompting questions and discussions; reading for pleasure and for information; writing across a range of forms, for real purposes and audiences.

Pat thought that the whole school benefited from the links developed with the community, the castle and the museum, and from the insights gained into the ways in which new resources introduced by the students, for example the brasses, could be used. The project was particularly helpful in demonstrating the effectiveness of a cross-curricular approach in delivering and assessing the National Curriculum Programmes of Study.

A subsequent fax from Pat read: 'Re Literacy Hour – are you pursuing any ideas about this – how teaching of history is likely to be affected? Next term's topic is 'When Gran was little' . . . (1950s) . . . nice . . . I'm going to try and deliver some elements of it through the literacy hour – any comments/suggestions appreciated.' So perhaps our next collaborative project is already beginning.

Pat also said that the opportunity to work intensively on one curriculum area with a group of history specialists over several days enabled teachers to observe the quality of teaching and learning which was taking place. They were impressed by the children's sustained interest and enthusiasm throughout the day, writing sometimes quite late in the afternoon, and felt that this had implications for future planning. Possibly blocks of such intensive input in foundation subjects can be a means to ensure depth and coherence and investigative approaches in a crowded and fragmented curriculum. Such units of work with students have implications for collaborative planning between schools and Initial Teacher Training courses as partnerships develop.

The children

Asked to sum up what the children had gained from the project, Pat said that they had been given opportunities to:

- develop knowledge, understanding and skills in history and English in ways which were meaningful, exciting and fun;
- work in different contexts, individually and collaboratively, in small groups, coming together as a class at the end; the underlying theme of a banquet gave cohesion and purpose;
- make things (the Design and Technology involved in making swords, shields and so on could have been tackled more thoughtfully, but the project gained impact because of the intensity).

The children also had lots of encouragement and praise, which both increased their self-esteem and enhanced the positive ethos of the classroom. To crown it all, an article on the project in the local newspaper was a source of great pride, pleasure and satisfaction to everyone.

The students

The students Alex, Alex, Anne, Laura and Sarra agreed that it was 'good to see a cross-curricular approach in action, and particularly to see the range of tasks all come together at the banquet'. They now felt confident to teach Key Element 3, interpretations of history, which they had previously found difficult at Key Stage 1; they said that by repeating and modifying each activity for each group they were able to refine their plans, and they appreciated the opportunity to work together and to talk to others about how the children performed on the different tasks. As for the tutor: 'how wonderful to get into a school and to work creatively with adults and children on a coherent unit of work and what a challenge to get beneath the assumptions that English and history are "obviously complementary" and explore precise contexts for proving it'.

After six months the students are going to meet again with Pat Etches and the children to find out what they have remembered about the Kendal Castle Project and why, as part of a larger research study investigating children's perceptions of their learning with trainee teachers, on different kinds of school placement.

References

Black, M. (1996) *The Medieval Cookbook*, London: British Museum Press.

School Curriculum and Assessment Authority (SCAA) (1995) *Planning the Curriculum at Key Stages 1 and 2*, London: SCAA Publications.

—— (1997a) *Standards at Key Stage 1, English and Mathematics: Report on the 1996 National Curriculum Assessment for 7 year olds*, London: SCAA Publications.

—— (1997b) *Expectations in History at Key Stage 1 and 2*, London: SCAA Publications.

Sendak, M. (1970) *Where the Wild Things Are*, Harmondsworth, Middx: Penguin.

12

'READ ALL ABOUT IT'

Using newspapers as an historical resource in an infant classroom

Janice Adams

Introduction

I can still remember the intense feeling of excitement as I sat in front of the television with my parents, late into the night, on 20 July 1969. Like millions of others, all around the world, we held our breath as Neil Armstrong slowly made his way on to the surface of the moon. I was eleven years old then, and for the first time had a real sense of having witnessed an historical event which I knew would be remembered and talked about by future generations.

The story of the first moon landing is one which I have told to many groups of children since then. It covers two areas of study in the current Key Stage 1 history curriculum: 'Pupils should be taught about the lives of different kinds of famous men and women; pupils should be taught about past events of different types' (DfE 1995: 74).

The work which forms the basis of this chapter was carried out initially with a class of year 1 children at the British School in The Netherlands, as part of a topic about 'Space', and then repeated with a year 2 class at Didsbury Road Primary School, Stockport, during a topic on 'The 1960s'. In discussing the work undertaken by the children I shall focus particularly on the impact of introducing the children to newspaper reports about the moon landings, and the opportunities which then arose for developing both reading and writing skills.

Learning about newspapers

Newspapers may not be an obvious choice of material for young children. They are, after all, written for an adult audience, and their content may be unsuitable for young readers. Yet they are also part of the daily experience of many children and can be a rich source of information about events past and present. With these points in mind, I collected five editions of a newspaper, printed during the previous fortnight, and used them as a basis for exploring the children's current knowledge and experience. It was soon evident that the children knew a great deal about the role of newspapers:

> It tells you the news.
> It's so you know what's happening everywhere.
> My mum reads the paper.

They were able to point out different features within the papers:

> That's a crossword – my dad likes doing them.
> That tells you what's on the telly.
> That's the weather, so you'll know if it's going to rain.

They also showed some awareness of why people might look in the paper for information. For example, when asked why there were sports pages in the paper, one child said:

> Well, if you couldn't go to the match, and you didn't know who'd won, or what happened, then you could read it in here and then you'd know.

We also talked about whether the stories in the newspapers were 'true' or 'made up'. The children were unanimous in agreeing that the newspapers were about things which had really happened. (I am sure that some adults would not agree with this. Issues of bias in reporting would certainly be a fruitful area for older children to explore, but probably too complex for most Key Stage 1 children to grasp.)

Front page news

Having given the children time to look through the papers and talk about what they had found, I then focused particularly on the front pages, asking the children if they noticed anything about the writing on those pages. They were quick to notice the headlines: 'That writing's really, really, really big!', though they struggled to offer an explanation for this. We then compared the front pages with some of the story books in the classroom and noticed that the newspaper was written in columns rather than right across the page.

We also looked at the photographs and other illustrations (including maps and diagrams) which were used to accompany the stories. The children were quite perceptive in some of their comments:

That man looks a bit cross. (*the picture was of a politician*)
They've got their picture in the paper 'cos they've just won and they're champions. (*about a front page picture of Manchester United*)

Finally, I focused the children's attention on to the date on each front page. When I asked: 'Which is today's paper?', some children guessed at random, but others looked at where the date was displayed in the classroom and used this to check the dates on the papers.

By this stage I had introduced the children to some general and specific points about newspapers. In particular, I had emphasised the idea that newspapers provided a written account of things which had happened that day, or not long previously, and had introduced some new vocabulary (*headline* and *column*) to describe particular features of the front page.

The process described above was the same for both the year 1 and year 2 groups. I have not treated their responses separately because I found few significant differences between the ideas expressed by each group during these introductory discussions. Both groups revealed a similar range of experience and understanding.

Newspapers as an historical resource

When I began planning the work, which was related to the history of space travel, I gathered a range of resources to use with the children. These included books, photographs and video material. I also made use of adults in school (including me) who could talk to the children about their memories of watching the moon landings on television. I also collected several newspaper reports from July 1969. One was an original front page, the rest were photocopies provided by the reference section of the local library.

The story of the moon landings was then presented to the children in several different ways. I began by reading accounts of the moon landings from children's reference books. These had the advantage of being presented in language which was accessible to the children, whilst giving them all of the key details of the event. This also ensured that they had some knowledge on which to draw when I introduced the newspaper reports.

The children responded with fascination to the newspaper accounts. The headlines were short and simple, and within the reading ability of virtually all of the children, as the following examples show:

MAN ON THE MOON (*Daily Mail*, 21 July 1969)

3.56 am : MAN STEPS ONTO THE MOON (*Guardian*, 21 July 1969)

There was also a strong visual element on all the front pages, with photographs of the astronauts and the lunar module, and maps of the lunar surface showing the landing site. As with the introductory work with current newspapers, I gave the children time to look and talk freely. Their initial comments revealed a grasp of the main events and people:

Look, look! Is it Neil Armstrong? He's coming down the ladder.
There's three astronauts going to the moon.
That says 'Man on the Moon' – it's like in my book about the moon.

The children were also clear about why this event was front page news:

It was the first time anyone had been to the moon so it was very important and . . . everyone might want to know what had happened.

At this stage, I began to guide the children to look more closely at the reports. The more fluent readers were able to read sections by themselves, otherwise I provided support by reading parts of each report to the children. The famous quotations 'the Eagle has landed' and 'one small step' featured in every report, and were immediately recognised by the children. We began to compare the newspaper reports with the reference books in the classroom. When I asked which accounts had been written first, some children were uncertain, but many realised that the newspaper reports had been written first:

This was written when it had really just happened.
This was in 1969, and that's a long time ago. (*pointing at the date on one paper*)

In a simple way, then, the children were beginning to distinguish between primary and secondary sources of information.

Young reporters

As indicated above, newspapers can be a valuable resource for history. But in learning about newspapers, children also gain valuable skills which are central to the English curriculum. They become familiar with the genre of reports, read for information, and have to distinguish between fiction and non-fiction. I decided to extend this developing awareness by using the moon landings as a stimulus for the children's writing. They were familiar with the idea of writing 'reports' from writing their own 'news' or accounts of things we had done at school. I gave the children the opportunity to create their own front page news stories about the first moon landing. The work was carried out over a period of several days.

I provided the children with thin 'columns' of paper on which to write their reports, explaining that they would be able to cut these up later and arrange them on their own 'front page'. I then provided strips of paper on which headlines were written, and plain rectangles in a variety of sizes which could be used for pictures. All these elements were combined and arranged by the children on their own A3 front page.

At each stage of the process, much was revealed about the children's knowledge of the historical event, and also about their ability to write in a style appropriate to a newspaper report. Across the two year groups, the children were able to stick to the facts of the story, as they remembered them. They were clearly able to distinguish between the imaginative 'space stories' which they had written earlier (tales of amazing encounters with aliens) and a report of an actual event. Some of the year 1 children's reports were brief, but to the point:

> Neil Armstrong landed on the moon. He felt happy. He put a flag on the moon. He walked on the moon.

Some year 1 children were also able to capture some of the feelings of excitement and apprehension which had been evident in the original reports. For example, one child wrote (Figure 12.1):

> Just as the module touched down, Neil Armstrong stepped out and everybody cheered because they had landed safely. Neil Armstrong made footprints and they will never blow away. They didn't know if their spacecraft was going to tip over because nobody has been on the moon before.

A number of children chose to quote the words spoken by Neil Armstrong as he stepped on to the surface of the moon. This led to much checking and rechecking as they looked back at the original reports or reference books to make sure that they had quoted correctly. They seemed to recognise that accuracy was an important part of a factual account.

The less fluent writers among the year 2 group produced reports similar to those described above. There were, however, some interesting examples from the more confident writers which revealed their growing ability to select language appropriate to the purpose. For example, one report (Figure 12.2) began:

> Today's news is the eagle has landed. Neil Armstrong has dared to put his foot on the moon. Neil said 'one small step for man, one giant leap for mankind.' Buzz Aldrin came down the ladder next.

183

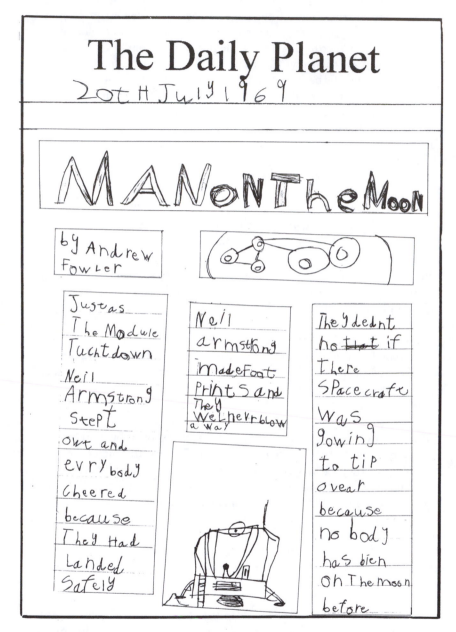

Figure 12.1 'Man on the moon'

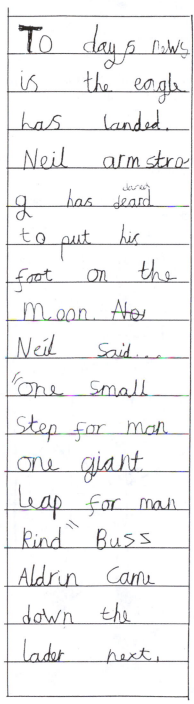

TO days news
is the eagle
has landed.
Neil armstro
g has deard
to put his
foot on the
moon. Now
Neil said...
"One small
step for man
one giant
leap for man
kind" Buss
Aldrin came
down the
lader next,

Figure 12.2 'Today's news'

Whilst another opened with:

> Big news. Spaceship lands on the moon.

Both extracts capture the tone and style of a news report very well.

In general, more of the older children tried to convey the excitement and emotion of the event, with references being made to the reactions of people watching and waiting back on earth:

> Meanwhile on earth people were excited about them up in space. Everyone was very happy.

> He put a flag on the moon, and everyone was gasping. They were safe and everyone cheered.

The year 2 children also tended to include greater detail in their accounts and used a wider range of vocabulary including terms such as 'orbit', 'lunar module', 'oxygen' and 'mission control'.

Figure 12.3 'Spaceman'

Making headlines

When they had finished their reports, the children selected headlines to accompany their stories. The majority of children were able to decide on a short but appropriate headline:

THE MOON LANDING

FOOTPRINTS ON THE MOON

THE FIRST STEP!

WALKING ON THE MOON

APOLLO 11 GETS TO THE MOON

ONE SMALL STEP

The range and variety were impressive, with children generally being keen to think up an original headline for their story. This activity also generated a lot of discussion, with ideas being considered and rejected: 'No! That's far too long!' By this stage, the children also had a much clearer idea of why there were headlines on the front pages:

> Well, you see the big writing first, and it tells you what the news is. It's so people will know what the story is about and then they'll want to read it.

It was evident that the opportunity to work on their own 'front page' had helped the children to develop their understanding of some of the ideas introduced when we had first looked at newspapers together. They were able to apply this understanding to their present task, and showed considerable confidence in selecting and rejecting material for their pages. There was also evidence of the application of skills from other work undertaken at the time. Several of the year 2 group, who had been learning about features of non-fiction texts, noticed the captions which accompanied the newspaper pictures and chose to add captions to their own illustrations. None of the year 1 children did this.

Putting the front page together

Having written reports and headlines, the children then had to decide how they wanted their front page to look. They decided where to place the text,

Figure 12.4 'Walking on the moon'

Figure 12.5 'Footsteps on the moon'

and selected paper of a suitable size for illustrations to fill the remaining spaces. This was certainly a challenging task, and the younger children needed some adult support in order to put their page together. The year 2 children were able to complete the final stage of the task much more independently. As with the choice of headlines, most of the children thought carefully about what kind of pictures were needed to accompany their stories. Thus, the paper with the headline FOOTPRINTS ON THE MOON also included a large picture of an astronaut leaving a long trail of footprints behind him (Figure 12.5).

On another occasion, when producing a 'front page', I provided the children with a prepared layout, largely to make the activity easier to manage with a large class. The columns and boxes for pictures were arranged on the paper below the headline, so that the children could work directly on to their 'page'. This is an application to Key Stage 1 of the technique of 'writing frames', which might also have been produced effectively on the computer. I was careful, however, to differentiate the spaces allocated to different children for writing and drawing, allowing more 'column' space for the more able writers. In the event, although the children lost the opportunity to design the final layout of their 'page', this was a simpler way of managing the activity and produced equally satisfying results.

With both groups, the level of perseverance and motivation was impressive. The children's interest was sustained over a period of several days, and they showed considerable care and effort in putting their papers together. They had also had a valuable opportunity to extend the range of their writing as the National Curriculum requires that:

Children should be helped to understand the value of writing as a means of remembering, communicating, organising and developing ideas and information, [and they should be] given opportunities to write in response to a variety of stimuli [and be] taught to organise and present their writing in different ways.

(DfE 1995: 9)

Conclusion

There were opportunities for developing children's historical knowledge and understanding throughout the project described above. Closely interwoven with this were valuable experiences across all three strands of the English curriculum. In Table 12.1, I will now pull together some of the key skills and concepts developed at each stage.

When attempting to evaluate work undertaken in the classroom, the question of what the children have learnt is always crucial. Some skills can be clearly identified and matched to attainment targets. But learning also involves some less tangible, but no less important, factors, such as enthusiasm, motivation and the self-esteem which results from completing a task well. Much of my satisfaction from the project stemmed from seeing the children's pleasure as they proudly showed their finished newspapers to their friends and parents. The year 1 group also began to bring newspaper

Table 12.1 Opportunities for history and English when using newspapers

English	History
Looking at newspapers	
Reading for information	Chronology: looking at dates
Distinguishing between fiction and non-fiction	Learning that newspapers are a record of events which occurred at a particular time
Participating in discussions; sharing ideas	
Looking at reports of the moon landings	
Reading for information	Finding information from written sources
Recalling and explaining the content of the reports	Learning about past events, and about people's responses to those events
Writing newspaper reports	
Planning, organising and reviewing writing	Communicating awareness and understanding of historical events
Writing in a particular form, incorporating characteristics of that form	

clippings to school, first of any current stories about space, then about other subjects. For quite some time, a small notice board in the corner of the classroom flourished with cuttings brought in and displayed by the children. Newspapers were no longer a purely adult province – the children had found that there were some parts that they found interesting too.

Reference

Department for Education (DfE) (1995) *History in the National Curriculum*, London: HMSO.

INDEX